D0500108

Leadership and Management of Volunteer Programs

James C. Fisher
Kathleen M. Cole

Leadership and Management of Volunteer Programs

A Guide for Volunteer Administrators

JOSSEY-BASS
A Wiley Company
www.josseybass.com

Published by

JOSSEY-BASS
A Wiley Company
989 Market Street
San Francisco, CA 94103-1741

www.josseybass.com

Jossey-Bass books and products are available through most bookstores. To contact Jossey-Bass directly, call (888) 378-2537, fax to (800) 605-2665, or visit our website at www.josseybass.com.

Substantial discounts on bulk quantities of Jossey-Bass books are available to corporations, professional associations, and other organizations. For details and discount information, contact the special sales department at Jossey-Bass.

We at Jossey-Bass strive to use the most environmentally sensitive paper stocks available to us. Our publications are printed on acid-free recycled stock whenever possible, and our paper always meets or exceeds minimum GPO and EPA requirements.

Library of Congress Cataloging-in-Publication Data

Fisher, James C.
    Leadership and management of volunteer programs: a guide for volunteer administrators / James C. Fisher, Kathleen M. Cole. — 1st ed.
        p.   cm. — (The Jossey-Bass nonprofit sector series)
    Includes bibliographical references (p.   ) and index.
    ISBN 1-55542-531-3 (alk. paper)
    1. Volunteers—Management. 2. Volunteers—United States—Management. I. Cole, Kathleen M., date. II. Title.
III. Series
HV35.F57   1993
361.3'7'068—dc20

92-44467
CIP

FIRST EDITION
HB Printing   10 9 8 7

The Jossey-Bass
Nonprofit Sector Series

Contents

Preface

Interest in professionalizing the practice of volunteer administration has increased dramatically in recent years. Under the leadership of the Association for Volunteer Administration (AVA) and with the guidance of organizations and individuals in the volunteer and nonprofit arena, the field increasingly emphasizes program and personnel management in addition to the development of technical skills.

Background

Most volunteer administrators are initiated into the profession through on-the-job or volunteer experience. Few have formal advanced training in the administration of volunteer programs, management theory, or personnel administration, yet they are expected to be competent at program planning and organization, staffing and directing, and supervising expenditures. Often the administrators feel overwhelmed by the magnitude of their job, which may stand in contrast to the degree of support provided by their organization. Much of the literature to date consists of how-to manuals, which offer practical suggestions and approaches derived from the experience of the authors, but do not adequately address the management challenges of the job.

This book discusses the profession of volunteer administration from a management perspective. *Leadership and Management of Volunteer Programs* provides an in-depth, multidisciplinary look at current research, theory, and literature from the field of management as they relate to volunteer administration. To illustrate the diverse and complex managerial functions of volunteer administrators, we describe specific situations from a range of settings, involving such populations as board members, regular volunteers, off-site volunteers, and short-term (or episodic) volunteers. The management tasks described are performed both by administrators of volunteer programs and by those with other titles who also have responsibility for the leadership or management of volunteers.

We encourage readers to examine the assumptions that undergird their practice, to understand the role that setting plays in shaping the administration of volunteers, and to consider alternative ways to view what they do and how they do it. Through this reflective process, readers should be able to identify strengths in their practice as well as areas requiring improvement. We also provide professionals with the management tools to articulate the scope of their responsibilities and consequently increase their resources and status.

Audience

Leadership and Management of Volunteer Programs was written for administrators in government, business, and nonprofit organizations, including religious and educational institutions, arts and cultural groups, social services, and other community-based agencies. It addresses the needs of volunteer practitioners at all levels, in both centralized (program management) and decentralized (personnel management) systems.

Current practitioners can use the book to develop their professional competencies through self-directed study or continuing education or to prepare for AVA certification. It also will serve as a comprehensive text for instructors and students in postgraduate courses in volunteer administration and nonprofit management. The material presented here is a valuable resource for leaders and staff of organizations that make use of volunteers, as well as for volunteers interested in entering this career field.

Finally, executive directors and board members who read this book will be exposed, many for the first time, to the broad scope of volunteer administration as well as to the advantages of professional management of the volunteer workforce. It is our hope that these executives will respond by increasing support and resources for the development of volunteer programs that mirror those described here.

Overview of the Contents

Chapter One examines the leadership and management roles of volunteer administrators. As leaders, they develop a vision for volunteer programs; as managers, they provide for the effective involvement of volunteers. Chapters Two and Three focus on staffing from two perspectives: the determination of roles for volunteer staff within the organization and the development of a systematic staff-selection process.

Chapter Four describes how volunteer administrators can develop a climate that motivates both new and experienced volunteers. It suggests activities to recognize volunteers' contributions and increase their retention. Chapter Five focuses on recruitment as a marketing challenge and encourages a planned effort to recruit volunteers from diverse racial and cultural backgrounds.

Chapter Six explores both formal and informal learning activities essential to volunteer development. It describes the value to an organization of investing in the training of its volunteer staff and provides information on the needs of learners. Chapter Seven gives an overview of the attitudes and skills required of supervisors of volunteers in order to increase volunteer retention and performance. The chapter offers guidelines for the design of a supervisory system that provides for adequate volunteer orientation and training, clearly communicated standards of performance, and staff support and guidance for volunteer efforts.

Chapter Eight shows how to evaluate the process, results, and impact of volunteer programs and suggests ways of developing evaluation plans to meet particular needs. Chapter Nine discusses the emergence of the profession and provides an overview of the philosophical and ethical foundations of the field of volunteer administration.

Resource A reproduces AVA's "Professional Ethics in Volunteer Services Administration," and Resource B lists the functional areas and performance criteria that make up the AVA competency-based certification program in volunteer administration.

Overall, the book describes the knowledge, skills, and abilities required of professional managers if volunteers are to be involved effectively in the work of organizations. It recognizes volunteer administration for what it has become: a management profession.

Acknowledgments

We are grateful for the encouragement we have received throughout our project from our colleagues and from members of the AVA. The functional areas and performance criteria described in the AVA competency-based certification program have served as a guide in the conceptualization of each chapter. AVA's leadership in establishing performance standards, ethical guidelines, and a certification program that recognizes experience and encourages reflection on practice has been invaluable in the development of volunteer administration as a profession. We have been particularly inspired by those who pioneered AVA's certification in volunteer administration; their vision significantly influenced our desire to produce this book. We especially acknowledge the support of David Hoffman, president of Family Service of Milwaukee, and express appreciation for his respect for the position of volunteer administrator within that agency and for his enabling Kathleen Cole to work on writing this book.

We also want to acknowledge the role of two groups in the maturation of our ideas. The first comprises the volunteers with whom we have worked, both as staff members and as fellow volunteers, throughout our personal and professional lives. They have been models of the depth of commitment to causes that improve the lives of people around the globe. The second group consists of the students in James Fisher's course in the leadership and management of volunteer programs at the University of Wisconsin–Milwaukee. They have been instrumental in the development of the topics covered here and have challenged assumptions not affirmed by their experience as volunteers or leaders of volunteer programs. Fisher's wife, Barbara, has supported this effort in a host of ways and joins the authors in anticipating the completion of the project.

Milwaukee, Wisconsin   James C. Fisher
February 1993   Kathleen M. Cole

The Authors

James C. Fisher is associate professor of adult and continuing education and director of the educational studies program at the University of Wisconsin-Milwaukee, where he has been a faculty member since 1981 in the department of administrative leadership. He received his B.A. degree (1955) in English from Maryville College, Tennessee, his M. Div. degree (1958) from Union Theological Seminary, New York City, his M.S. degree (1974) in adult education and his Ph.D. degree (1979) in urban education from the University of Wisconsin-Milwaukee. Fisher has had extensive experience as a staff member in a volunteer organization and as a volunteer for various community and education projects. He is a member of the board of trustees for Carroll College, president-elect of the board of directors for Literacy Service of Wisconsin, and an executive committee member for the National Commission of Professors of Adult Education. The Milwaukee Council for Adult Learning has honored him with its Distinguished Service Award. Fisher is the author of numerous articles, book chapters, and papers on adult education. He is coeditor of the *Encyclopedia of School Administration and Supervision* (1988) with R. A. Gorton and G. T. Schneider.

Kathleen M. Cole is currently employed with two organizations: with Family Service of Milwaukee, as manager of program development, and with the United Way of Door County, as executive director. She received her B.A. degree (1976) in conservation from the University of Wisconsin-Madison, and her M.S. degree (1988) in the administrative leadership of adult education programs from the University of Wisconsin-Milwaukee. She has thirteen years of experience in volunteer administration, including positions at a volunteer center, a natural history museum, a social service agency, and the United Way. She is an active member of the Association for Volunteer Administration (AVA), where she has provided leadership at the local, regional, and national levels. She achieved AVA certification in volunteer administration in 1985 and was recertified in 1990. Cole is coauthor of "Valuing Volunteers: A Naturalistic Approach," published in *The Journal of Volunteer Administration* (1989, with James Fisher).

Leadership and Management of Volunteer Programs

Part One

Volunteers
in the
Organization

1

The Volunteer Administrator as Leader and Manager

A re administrators of volunteer services in essence managers like other managers, or is their role more similar to that of various kinds of volunteers in an organization? The answer to this question often depends on how the role of volunteer administrators develops within a particular organization. Ellis and Noyes (1990) describe three historic categories of volunteer leadership: first, the member of a volunteer group selected to be the leader, like the president of a service club; second, the paid staff person who supervises volunteers as a secondary responsibility, like a nurse or teacher who also manages volunteers in a ward or classroom or the human resource leader in a business who also oversees the volunteer literacy program; third, the staff person, full or part-time, paid or unpaid, whose primary function is to coordinate the work of volunteers.

Although in practice most of the responsibilities discussed in this book are undertaken by persons in each of these three categories, those in the third category are most likely to identify themselves as professional administrators of volunteer services and to them the conceptualization here will be most familiar.

Schindler-Rainman (1988, p. 20.4) describes the development of this administrator's role in the following way: "It is clear that a new profession is emerging in the volunteer world. It is the volunteer administrator, director, or coordinator, who oversees and supervises a volunteer program. . . . The volunteer administrator may be the executive director of an agency or organization utilizing a large number of volunteers in order to carry out its services. Or the volunteer director may be a middle-management person within an organization in charge of the volunteer program."

Since the 1960s this position has established itself as a profession requiring particular management skills; nevertheless, widespread disparity still exists. In some instances, administrators of volunteer programs may have other major responsibilities within an organization, allowing only a portion of their time to be devoted to the volunteer program. In other cases, organizations may fail to consider the manager of volunteer programs as being on the same level as other program managers. Or a volunteer administrator may be promoted from within the ranks of volunteers, the presumption being that she will gain the management skills necessary through volunteering or by learning on the job. In other instances, volunteer administrators may lack the professional identity and particular training in management or administration required of other managers. Finally, organizations may fail to articulate in a volunteer administrator's job description the management skills required. This diversity of perception and practice notwithstanding, the role of volunteer administrator involves a range of specific leadership and management skills.

Wilson (1984) observes that voluntary organizations are often managed by persons who are trained in the helping professions but have little administrative training and little experience managing organizations. In contrast, the fastest-growing segment of the volunteer force consists of professionals accustomed to working within competently managed organizations and able to recognize ineffectual program leadership and management skills.

In a study of the organizational needs of voluntary organizations, Miller (1986) found that the most frequently identified problems were recruiting, training, and effectively managing volunteers; approximately 40 percent of the needs fell into these categories. Other problems commonly identified were associated with program planning and development, management of organizational processes, and the development of organizational structures. Wilson and Miller both point to the need to enhance the quality of management available for the administration of volunteer programs.

Like other emerging professions, the profession of volunteer administration has been forced to grapple with a precise definition of the responsibilities involved. Among those articulated in the literature and by practicing professionals are the role of the administrator as the leader and direction setter of the volunteer effort, as the manager of volunteer programs and personnel, as the advocate for volunteers within an organization, as the key communication link between the organization and its volunteers, and as a raiser of funds to support the volunteer program. Although job descriptions may include any or all of these responsibilities, the twin roles of leadership and management emerge as paramount.

Kotter (1990, pp. 3-4) defines leadership as the "process that helps direct and mobilize people and/or their ideas" and management as the means to assist a complex organization to achieve consistent results. Although the functions of leader and manager may be clearly distinguished from each other, leaders are nevertheless called on to manage and managers are expected to lead. Both roles are critical to the success of a program. Kotter (1990, p. 5) further explains that both leadership and management involve "deciding what needs to be done, creating networks of people and relationships that can accomplish an agenda, and then trying to ensure that those people actually get the job done."

Leadership Responsibilities

Key leadership responsibilities include setting direction, encouraging others to share that agenda, and inspiring others to help accomplish it.

In a study of ninety effective leaders, Bennis (1984) defined four competencies discernible in each of his subjects: focusing on commitment to a vision or an agenda; communicating and interpreting the vision so that others align themselves with it; maintaining a reliable, consistent posture; and knowing one's strengths and deploying them effectively. In addition, the administrator of volunteer programs is often required to serve as an advocate for the volunteer effort within an organization, removing obstacles so that the vision may be articulated and achieved.

The Leader as Visionary

The role of setting direction establishes the administrator of volunteer programs as the visionary, the one who looks to the future to determine client needs and corresponding volunteer programs, to assure that the organization will over time respond in an increasingly effective and efficient way, and to point out important milestones that must be passed on the way from the present program to the one envisioned. The importance of the visionary cannot be overestimated. The administrator of volunteer programs is one of few in many organizations likely to possess such a vision. Without it, a program may do little more than react to the needs presented. Vision is particularly important for nonprofit organizations because most lack a "bottom line," rely heavily on unpaid personnel and reward them with intangible benefits. A clearly articulated vision defines for an organization's volunteers both the nature of their responsibilities and the level of performance to which they may aspire.

Such visions have neither a standard form nor a specific substance. They are idiosyncratic, depending on the visionary, the nature of the program, and the internal and external environments of the organization. Often they redress present deficiencies: better facilities, more productive fundraising, a larger group of volunteers, a program that commands the respect of others in the community, a broader service area, more skilled leadership, or a higher level of performance. Sometimes the vision boldly charts a new direction: a storefront literacy program sees the workplace as the new focus of its mission; a social service agency relocates its program for child-abuse prevention from community organizations and churches to schools; a downtown church redefines its global mission in order to concentrate on the elderly and homeless within a six-block area; a national health organization develops a service initiative to match its research program. A vision may also articulate with new clarity an organization's direction and mission, which may previously have been cloaked in ambiguities and conflicting assumptions. Regardless of its substance, the vision serves as a beacon guiding an organization to its future purpose and simultaneously amplifying the meaning of its present program.

Frequently, a vision for the entire organization is held by the board, executive, and other leaders. In that case, the administrator of volunteer programs supports the organization's vision and participates in its achievement as it involves the volunteer program. However, the volunteer administrator must also envision the future of the volunteer programs within the organization and develop the means through which the vision is realized.

A leader's responsibility for setting direction, for holding forth a vision, places the volunteer administrator in the position of change agent. The vision challenges the status quo and makes complete contentment with the present unthinkable. The tensions between present and future, between what is and what might be, between current problems and future hopes, require a leader who can regulate these tensions as the organization moves toward its future.

The vision is both the product of the organization's culture and the creator of that culture. No vision is separated from an organization's history or environment; it articulates an organization's values, communicates its priorities, and inspires behavior that reflects them. The following case illustrates how envisioning change influences program practice.

> The new executive director of an adult education center inherited a board of directors consisting mostly of volunteers at the center. Although the board members supported the center through generous contributions of time and money, they lacked experience in public relations and fundraising. As a result, the organization's program was limited by its inability to expand its resource base.
>
> The new executive envisioned a board with more diverse members who would have access to a variety of financial resources and possess expertise in fundraising and public relations. To achieve the vision, she worked with the board to identify proficiencies needed by new board members, to cultivate interested persons who possessed these proficiencies, and to present three of these individuals each year for

board membership. After three years, the board members had more diverse backgrounds and expertise in fundraising and public relations than previous members.

Sharing the Vision

The second role of the leader is to share the vision in such a way that it becomes the vision of others, paid staff and volunteers alike; in aligning themselves with the vision, they come to accept it as their agenda, articulate it to others, and incorporate it into their work. The vision must belong to those who have been enlisted to achieve it. Kotter (1990, p. 60) advocates "communicating the direction as often as possible . . . to all those people . . . whose help or cooperation is needed; doing so, whenever possible, with simple images or symbols or metaphors that communicate powerfully without clogging already overused communication channels and without requiring a lot of scarce managerial time." Organizations have used badges, banners, logos, and slogans to capture the essence of a vision and to disseminate it. As others accept the vision, it becomes an important bridge between the expectations and goals of the organization and the needs of the individual volunteers; it also becomes an important component of their loyalty to the organization or cause.

Furthermore, the vision adds a future dimension to the present-time parameters of a program, often saving it from being completely submerged by the needs of the present and offering to its constituents a broad view of the organization's role. New meaning is given to volunteer work when the volunteer is aware that the service provided in the present is the result of earlier visions and that future volunteers will continue the work being done in the present.

Fulfilling the Vision

The third role of the leader is to inspire others to achieve the vision and to use it to influence present and future practice in an organization. This task necessitates a joint effort by both paid and unpaid staff to overcome barriers to the vision within the organization and its environment. By investing others with important responsibilities in realizing the vision and facilitating the necessary changes (however incremental), an administrator can counteract possible indifference and alienation. It is virtually impossible for a single leader, especially an administrator of volunteer programs, to bring to fruition a major change without the involvement of others. Pearce (1982, p. 391) rightly affirms that "leaders of voluntary organizations are probably more dependent on their volunteer followers than are leaders in any other type of organization." An effective leader will use the organizational structure, collaborate with existing groups, develop special coalitions, and prepare others for change.

Often the leader is most effective working within an organization's informal structure through personal relationships and interactions with informal work groups and through coalitions with informal leaders. This structure provides the communication links and the collaborative relationships that allow the leader to involve others in the vision; these links are not always available within an organization's official chain of command and formal structure.

A good leader of volunteers is able to encourage them to perform without getting in their way and to provide the necessary tools and support.

An inner-city social service agency had a long history of involving volunteers in the delivery of its family-life education programs. Although the agency was located in an impoverished urban area, most of its educational programs were conducted in suburban neighborhoods by highly educated white females from middle- and upper-class families.

The agency developed a new strategic plan that mandated increased resources for servicing families in the agency's immediate neighborhood. The volunteer administrator seized this opportunity to gain support for a peer-education program with leadership from the indigenous client population.

Both paid staff and current volunteers were involved in discussions about how the new plan would affect the current volunteer program. Paid staff attended a national training program to prepare them to train volunteers as peer facilitators. Current volunteers were invited to be trained; six agreed to participate in the new program in the central city. A targeted recruitment drive resulted in the involvement of six minority individuals from the agency's neighborhood.

As the first new family-life education programs were conducted, the volunteer administrator asked paid and volunteer staff to identify participants who demonstrated leadership potential and a sound understanding of the parenting principles being taught. These successful completers were offered the opportunity to be trained as peer facilitators. Local foundations supported the program with funding adequate to provide training and supervision for the new peer facilitators, stipends during their training, and childcare reimbursement.

The vision of this volunteer administrator clearly required the support of agency decision makers, paid and volunteer staff, and local funding sources. She gained this support by involving others in implementing the plan and by being sensitive to ways in which the volunteer program could support and participate in the organization's vision.

Effective leadership moves an organization toward fulfillment of its vision and empowers those who participate in that effort. Bennis (1991, p. 15) describes empowerment as the "collective effect of leadership." With empowerment, people feel like an important part of a team or community, they make a contribution to the organization's success, they value learning and competence, and they find that the work challenges and energizes them. Empowerment adds to volunteers' sense of significance and value to the organization and emphasizes their capabilities.

Neither the leaders nor the followers are involved without risk; every effort to articulate and build a new future is subject to criticism, rejection, resistance, and failure. But the rewards are equal to the risk as the quality of the program and the loyalty and commitment of the paid and unpaid staff are enhanced. Effective leadership by the volunteer administrator results in a highly motivated volunteer corps focused on the values and outcomes implicit in the vision.

The Leader as Advocate

Leadership does not just mean looking to the future however. One important role of the administrator of volunteer programs is to be sensitive to those situations where volunteers are portrayed in a way that fails to reflect their commitment or their competence accurately. Another role is to be an advocate for policies and procedures that provide satisfying benefits and appropriate recognition to volunteers. Despite the important contribution that volunteers make to many organizations, their value is frequently questioned; and often the volunteer program is subject to misunderstanding, denigration, and diminishing or fluctuating organizational support. As a result, administrators of volunteer programs are called on with surprising frequency to stand for and with volunteers on both an individual and a group basis and to promote their acceptance within an organization. The advocacy role requires correcting misinformation, confronting inappropriate attitudes, and responding to inappropriate requests for volunteer services. It also requires interpreting the role of volunteers and their relation to the mission of the organization and teaching various constituencies how to work with them and support them.

Ellis (1986, p. 1) suggests that one of the primary roles of the volunteer administrator is to advocate for substantive support for the volunteer program from the organization's top administrators. "Lack of support is not due to malice or unwillingness to be of help, but is rather due to the failure of executives to understand what is really needed of them." By ensuring support in the form of money; an organizational philosophy that includes volunteer involvement; paid staff job descriptions that include volunteer management as an area of responsibility; and paid positions that allocate time for volunteer support, supervision, and training, a top executive can provide concrete assistance to the volunteer program. The volunteer administrator who works toward increased executive understanding of the needs of the volunteer program and involves executives in program planning and evaluation is setting the stage for program success.

One important aspect of the advocacy role is serving as a communication link between the organization in general, its board, administration, and staff, and the components or units that involve volunteers. At this critical juncture, the volunteer administrator funnels information from the organization to volunteers and from the volunteer program to the remainder of the organization. Organizational information serves to remind volunteers of the larger context in which they work and of the expectations of the organization that they are fulfilling; information about the volunteer program informs the organization and its publics of the important contribution volunteers are making to the achievement of the organization's mission.

Managerial Responsibilities

Having the volunteer administrator as a member of the management team of an organization is a fairly recent development. Models of volunteer management have been drawn from program, personnel, and business management models. These models have changed over time under the influence of prevailing cultural ideologies, economic trends, workplace philosophies, labor shortages and surpluses, and global competition. Some business-management models assume that a distance exists between managers and staff, that managers alone bear responsibility for outcomes, and that close control of staff by managers is necessary to ensure productivity. Others assume that managers and staff have similar interests, are distinguished not by distance but by job diversification, and bear responsibility equally for productive outcomes. The literature describing the management of volunteer programs reflects a diversity of approaches: some tend to emphasize similar accountability for volunteers and paid staff; others focus on differences between volunteers and paid staff and call for models of volunteer management that address the unique needs and features of organizations involving volunteers.

Classic models of management have described how persons must behave in a bureaucratic organization characterized by hierarchical authority and division of work. In such an organization, all persons report to another, and the mission of the organization is divided into components and assigned to subunits. Tasks required to administer such an organization were originally identified as planning, organizing, commanding, coordinating, and controlling. Later staffing, directing, reporting, and budgeting were added to the list, which provided for seven administrative tasks: "planning, organizing, staffing, directing, coordinating, reporting, and budgeting" (Hoy and Miskel, 1982, p. 3). Over time, the interpersonal relationships of those involved in the workplace, their motivation and satisfaction, came to be emphasized rather than the structural elements of management contained in the classic model. Later a model that emphasized the interaction between the human elements of an organization and the organization's formal structure evolved.

Peter Drucker (1989) credited nonprofit organizations with providing leadership in the practice of management through the use of the following: clearly focused mission statements, careful placement of personnel, providing training on a continuing basis, diligent use of resources, managing on the basis of clearly stated objectives, and expecting paid and unpaid staff to be accountable for their performance. Drucker notes that in crucial areas, such as strategy, the effectiveness of the board of directors, and the motivation and productivity of knowledgeable workers, American nonprofits "are practicing what most American businesses only preach" (p. 88).

The classic administrative tasks take different shapes depending on an institution's size, purpose, and environment. Cronk (1982) defines the responsibilities of directors of volunteers as follows:

1. *Planning:* Determining in advance what will be done.
   Develop goals and objectives.
   Implement board policies.
2. *Organizing:* Determining how work will be divided and accomplished.
   Interview.

Develop job descriptions.

Use community resources.

Develop resources for volunteer programs.

3. *Staffing:* Assuring there are qualified people to fill needed positions.

Identify needs and opportunities for volunteer service.

Utilize various recruitment techniques.

Schedule volunteers.

4. *Directing:* Getting people to accomplish tasks assigned to them by motivating, communicating and leading.

Provide orientation and training.

Supervise volunteers.

Develop volunteer recognition program.

Establish lines of supervision.

5. *Controlling:* Assuring that established goals and objectives are being met.

Monitor volunteer program.

Provide on-going evaluation of program and job performance.

6. *Interpersonal roles:* Serving as a figurehead, leader, liaison.

Work creatively within the structure.

Promote volunteerism.

Serve as a liaison between agency and community.

Assure communication between staff and volunteers.

Maintain good public relations.

7. *Informational roles:* Serving as a message center, monitoring and disseminating information, serving as a catalyst.

Enlist support of staff for volunteers.

Maintain records.

Be knowledgeable about trends and issues.

8. *Decision maker:* Allocating resources, negotiating, acting as group consultant.

"Hire," fire, and assign volunteers.

Identify service gaps.

Cronk concludes that directors of volunteers have classic management responsibilities requiring management skills and behaviors and are evaluated on the basis of management criteria.

Approaches to Volunteer Management

Volunteer programs tend to be organized according to one of two basic approaches: the personnel management approach or the program management approach. Each of these approaches may be observed in organizations that involve volunteers and employ the services of an administrator of volunteer programs. The personnel management approach is typically used when the volunteer program is scattered throughout the organization; the program management approach usually occurs when the volunteer program is central to an organization's principal purpose. Thus, the use of one approach or the other is usually the by-product of program organization; neither is inherently superior to the other. However, each requires a different system of organization of volunteers and different relationships to other personnel and units.

Personnel Management. In the personnel management approach, the volunteer administrator works closely with the staff of various departments or programs to determine the types of assistance required and the roles that may be performed by volunteer staff. The volunteer administrator guides the paid staff in the development and design of volunteer roles and the preparation of job descriptions for volunteers. She then recruits and interviews volunteers, arranges for a second interview or a meeting between new volunteers and the paid staff with whom they will work, handles the final screening process as needed, and provides new volunteers with an orientation to the organization. Examples of organizations using this approach are hospitals, museums, zoos, social service agencies, theater companies, educational institutions, and others where volunteers have many different responsibilities throughout the organization.

In this approach, the volunteer program is decentralized; once the volunteer is placed in a particular position, the paid staff supervisor or other professional in that unit arranges for training, ongoing supervision, and evaluation. The volunteer's principal accountability is to the paid staff supervisor or other paid professional in the unit where the volunteer position is located. The volunteer administrator serves as a consultant to the paid staff in the development of volunteer training curricula and in the use of supervisory techniques, record keeping, performance reviews, and problem-solving with volunteers but does not supervise volunteers directly or provide for their training.

In the following illustration, the role of the volunteer administrator in a decentralized setting is clarified:

A volunteer administrator for a large metropolitan zoo found that most paid staff who supervised volunteers contacted her about volunteer performance problems and expected her to intervene directly. She was concerned about volunteer/staff relations as well as the integrity of the volunteer program and responded promptly to their pleas for assistance. In most cases, however, her relationships with the volunteers in question was limited. After the initial interview, orientation, and placement had been completed, training and supervision were handled within the department in which volunteers worked. Therefore, her ability to address effectively the problems related to volunteers in departments would always be minimal.

The volunteer administrator was forced to reassess her responsibility to the organization. First, she redefined her role as the organization's internal consultant for volunteers. She contacted all supervisory staff to assess their capacity to conduct performance reviews and address performance problems involving volunteers. She then scheduled a series of training sessions to prepare them to handle difficult situations concerning volunteer staff. As part of the training, she discussed her new job description and described the ways in which she could provide guidance and support to the professional staff in their supervision of volunteers.

As this example shows, rather than directly intervening, the volunteer administrator in a decentralized system helps supervisory staff develop the skills and knowledge required to work with volunteers.

Program Management. The program management approach is used when volunteers are involved in one or more distinct activities central to the mission of the organization. Volunteers in this type of program are typically supervised directly by the volunteer administrator, as they provide direct service to clients. Examples of organizations using this approach are youth programs, literacy services, hospital fundraising groups, and membership organizations—all those where volunteers are involved in delivery of the services that constitute the major portion of the organization's mission.

As a program manager, the volunteer administrator is typically responsible for all management tasks including job design, recruitment, interviewing, screening, orientation, training, supervision, recordkeeping, and evaluation. The volunteer administrator may perform these tasks or may delegate portions of them to experienced volunteers, to other staff members, or, as in the case of training or program evaluation, to an outside expert.

In the following illustration, a program that involved large numbers of volunteers developed a new organizational scheme:

A learning center for older adults devised a system whereby volunteers were organized into specific program areas: teaching, fundraising, public relations, clerical support. Each area was headed by a volunteer chairperson. The center hired a part-time volunteer administrator who was responsible for assisting the executive director in developing the program; overseeing the volunteer program; and recruiting, placing, orienting, training, supervising, and providing support services to all volunteers in the organization.

In this illustration, the administrator of volunteer programs bears responsibility for the program of the center as well as for staffing the program with volunteers.

In the program management approach, the volunteer administrator is a program developer as well as the leader of volunteer efforts integral to the organization's program delivery. In the personnel management approach, the volunteer administrator recruits, selects, and places volunteers and trains paid staff to work with them. In both approaches, the responsibilities of the volunteer administrator usually include job design, recruitment, interviewing, orientation, and recognition. The purpose and structure of an organization will determine which of these approaches is more appropriate. Each organization must examine its structure and staffing patterns to determine the appropriate relationship between volunteers and the organization, the paid staff, and the volunteer administrator.

Functions of the Volunteer Administrator

In the development of its performance-based assessment program for the certification of volunteer administrators, the Association for Volunteer Administration (AVA) identified four functional areas in which each volunteer administrator should be able to demonstrate competence: program planning and organization; staffing and directing; controlling; and agency, community, and professional relations (Rehnborg, 1982). The AVA competencies are described in Resource B.

Program Planning and Organization. The administrator of volunteer programs bears key responsibility for the planning directly related to the volunteer program and should be an integral part of the team that plans for the entire organization. Planners begin with a clear mission statement, identify programs needed to attain the mission goals, consider the organizational structure needed to accomplish its purpose, develop objectives that describe the minimum performance level, identify resources necessary to accomplish the plan, and describe the evaluation procedure by which the completed plan will be judged. The planners acknowledge the external and internal environments of the organization or program and address elements of those environments that affect the plan. Most organizations possess a planning document that articulates short-term and long-term objectives for the organization and its programs; it defines clearly and succinctly the business of the organization and how that business is performed. Planning documents are revised periodically as circumstances and needs change and as the organization is challenged to redefine its purpose. Optimally the planning document will be the product of participatory decision making by the board, the paid staff, volunteers, clients, and others who may be affected by the program.

A chief responsibility of the administrator of volunteer programs is to translate organizational plans into goals and objectives for volunteer achievement, timetables, position descriptions, and staffing and budget plans for specific organizational units. In this way, each unit is involved in the implementation of the organizational plan and policy. These operational plans then become the basis for recruitment, selection, placement, and fundraising. In organizations that involve volunteers in a decentralized fashion to implement various parts of their program as well as in those that focus the work of volunteers on their direct service mission, an integral part of planning is the delineation, both at a policy and at a service-delivery level, of the responsibility of volunteers and of their relationship to the organization's mission and to its paid staff.

In addition to implementing the organizational plan, the administrator of volunteer programs provides important information and data for the planning process in order to help the organization focus on client needs. This responsibility may involve the administrator in assessing the needs of the present client population as well as in identifying and describing accurately other client groups who may benefit from the services of the organization.

Staffing and Directing. An important management function—some would argue the most important—of the volunteer administrator is that subsumed under the broad heading of personnel. Planning for the efficient and effective use of volunteers, designing volunteer positions, recruiting and screening volunteers, preparing them for assignments, placing them in positions, and supervising and over-seeing their work are integral to this function. In effect, the personnel function provides the human resources for the implementation of the plan. Other equally important activities consist of creating and presenting orientation and training programs, continually recognizing and motivating volunteers, developing service options for volunteers, and dealing with dissatisfied or troublesome volunteers.

Geber (1991, p. 26), in discussing personnel management, affirms that managing people is the same whether they are paid staff or volunteers: "They all must be managed with the basic understanding that they need clear objectives, feedback and opportunity for input." However, Pearce (1983) affirms that investment in organizational goals is greater for unpaid than for paid staff.

Controlling. The purpose of this management role is to monitor performance and assure quality of service. It consists of two major functions. The first is program evaluation, in which the degree to which goals have been accomplished, objectives have been met, and activities have produced the anticipated results is assessed. In demonstrating the efficiency and effectiveness of a program, the volunteer administrator assumes the role of evaluator of volunteer programs, involving others in the development and utilization of the evaluation plan, gathering and analyzing data integral to the evaluation, and reporting (formally or informally) the outcome of the examination of the program. Evaluation is usually carried out simultaneously with the program in order to monitor it, and evaluation is also conducted at the conclusion of the program for a final report.

The second major control function is responding to the findings of the evaluation. The volunteer administrator as controller is charged with modifying programs and personnel when the desired outcomes are not being achieved. Thus the responsibility for program oversight and management—that programs be carried out according to schedule, that they achieve objectives and thereby contribute to the organization's mission, that they serve clients in ways described in the program plan, that their impact is commensurate with that anticipated—falls to the volunteer administrator.

Should the program fail to produce results according to the plan, the volunteer administrator is responsible for modifying the program to meet expectations.

Record keeping provides the manager with the data needed to perform these control functions. The data bank for a volunteer organization ought to include information about all volunteers— their responsibilities, their training, the extent of their service—as well as provide information about the cost and benefits of programs. A detailed discussion of the data that support control and evaluation decisions may be found in Chapter Eight.

Agency, Community, and Professional Relations. The administrator of volunteer programs operates within several contexts—the organization, the community, and the profession—and performs various tasks within these contexts—enhancing interpersonal relations, providing group leadership, and facilitating organizational change. Furthermore, the administrator of volunteer programs is expected to be knowledgeable about the history and philosophy of volunteerism, the profession of volunteer administration, and the external regulations affecting the use of volunteers.

In operational terms, the volunteer administrator must represent the profession, use good interpersonal skills, and use effective communication skills. The volunteer administrator may be one of the few in an organization knowledgeable about the scope and significance of the volunteer movement and trends in the availability and use of volunteers. The volunteer administrator as a professional enhances the image of volunteers and defines the unique service volunteers are able to provide within an organization.

The volunteer administrator is also expected to develop positive interpersonal relationships: to provide leadership in building trust among individuals and groups, to engage in problem-solving activities, and to use conflict-resolution strategies. In so doing, the volunteer administrator has ample opportunity to model good questioning, active-listening, and feedback skills. These human relations skills, sometimes lacking among professionals trained in other disciplines, often help make the volunteer administrator invaluable to an organization.

Within the organization in which the volunteer administrator functions, especially if the volunteer program is decentralized, he often serves as the important communication link between the volunteer effort and the program delivered by paid staff, between the organization and the clients, and between the unpaid and paid staffs. In the larger sense, the volunteer administrator serves as the representative of the volunteer program to the organization, as the advocate of volunteers within the organization, and as the ambassador of the volunteer effort to the community. He is the link between various aspects of the program, its providers, its funders, and its clients.

Many organizations that use volunteers sometimes have special communication needs: volunteers may function in highly individualized or isolated circumstances, they may work when other staff members are not present or they may work at remote locations, or they may function in situations requiring high levels of confidentiality. Furthermore, many organizations rely heavily on the services of occasional and short-term volunteers. In each case, the administrator of volunteer programs may need to develop special relationships with these persons in order to maintain active communication.

Budgeting and Fundraising. The responsibility of administrators of volunteer programs for budgeting and fundraising depends to a large extent on the degree to which the administrators bear organizationwide responsibility or bear responsibility for the volunteer program within the larger organization. When administrators are responsible solely for volunteer programs, they are ordinarily charged with managing only that section of the organization's budget that supports the volunteer program. This budget contains funds for the volunteer administrator's position; office; recruitment, training, and recognition efforts; and other support services for volunteers.

In this instance, the principal functions of the volunteer administrator are to understand the organization's budget (in order to assist in fundraising and to interpret the budget to various constituencies) and to manage that portion of the budget directly related to the volunteer program. Effective budget management involves monitoring expenditures and income as well as apportioning budget items among various programs or activities. For example, a volunteer administrator should be able to identify what portion of any line item goes to specific programs. Effective budget management consists of allocating resources for the greatest impact within the parameters given.

In contrast, when volunteer administrators bear organizationwide or centralized responsibility, they may organize and carry out the fundraising effort as well. Managing fundraising entails the same basic tasks as managing the volunteer effort: planning and organizing, staffing and directing, controlling, and relating. Fundraising may also involve a group of volunteers, such as an auxiliary or friends' group, whose main purpose is to raise funds for an organization.

Every fundraising effort begins with a plan or plans: most plans focus specifically on the following year but identify adaptations, such as new populations to be solicited, for future years. At a minimum, the fundraising plan consists of objectives, activities, a time line, and the assignment of responsibilities; the plan also distinguishes funds to be raised through general solicitation, through special events, and through grants. More elaborate plans describe campaign literature and include lists of members, individual donors, corporate donors, foundations, government programs, and other sources of funds. The plan also details the nature of the contacts to be made: who will be contacted by phone, in person, by mail, or by a combination of these, by whom, and by what date.

The plan also coordinates the needs of the organization with the priorities of the various funding sources: particular components of the program are identified as appropriate for special requests. Grant applications are developed according to the schedule and objectives of potential funders. For example, developing a training program to assist telephone crisis-line volunteers in addressing problems with new street drugs may fit within the priorities of a local foundation interested in improving the welfare of young people and may therefore be the subject of a grant application.

The development of the plan itself is the work of some combination of paid staff and volunteers. Coordinating the efforts of both paid and unpaid staff plus administrators and board members begins with work on the plan; it continues as other staff and volunteers are incorporated into its development and implementation. In some organizations a volunteer is charged with chairing the annual fundraising effort; in others, the chief administrative officer performs that function. In either event, tasks to be performed need to be identified: recruiting and training volunteer workers, providing oversight, and maintaining the effort according to the plan and schedule. The need for recognition for paid and unpaid staff who participate in the fundraising effort should not be overlooked.

Furthermore, the fundraising program entails control tasks in much the same way other programs do. The program must be monitored so that it is implemented according to the plan; data must be gathered in order to assess the program's effectiveness and efficiency; and modifications must be made when necessary.

Perhaps none of the tasks of volunteer management is as important to fundraising as maintaining interpersonal relationships. Contributions of money and time are expressions of belief and trust in the work of an organization: donors believe that the work is important to do, and they trust that their contributions are being well used in that work. Although printed material may extol the virtue of an organization or its program and present valuable information, it cannot by itself nurture the belief and trust so valuable in fundraising. The involvement of the administrator of volunteer programs and volunteers themselves both as contributors and in relating to other donors is a critical resource for every organization.

Because the management tasks for effective fundraising are similar to those for effective program administration, it is common for fundraising to become integrated into an organization's program. Organizations are challenged to maintain an appropriate balance between the achievement of their mission through program activities and the need to support that program through successful fundraising.

Conclusion

Competition for all resources, whether the funding resources of donors or the personnel resources of volunteers, requires strong leadership and sound management. Scarce human and financial resources compel organizations to use them efficiently. Few characteristics of an organization convey its commitment to its mission as much as the way it administers its program and its determination to be a good steward of its resources. A well-run program communicates seriousness of purpose to its participants and encourages them to share its vision and to provide the time and energy necessary for its implementation. Good leaders and managers welcome the scrutiny of others and convince those both outside and inside the organization of its effectiveness and efficiency.

2

Developing the Role
of Volunteers
in the Organization

A challenge faced by most volunteer administrators is ensuring that the work of volunteers contributes to the achievement of organizational goals. For a volunteer program to make a difference, it is necessary, first, that the right volunteers have the right roles and the right responsibilities, and, second, that volunteers and paid staff work together in the pursuit of common goals. The skillful achievement of these two objectives is fundamental to the success of any volunteer program and therefore is of primary concern to each volunteer administrator.

In a period of increasing need for volunteer services and decreasing time available from volunteers, the fundamental questions of where and how to involve volunteer staff most effectively become vitally important. Organizations cannot afford to place volunteers in positions that do not directly enhance organizational effectiveness or in programs characterized by poor relationships or conflict between paid and volunteer staff. Friction between these two groups diverts valuable time and energy from the achievement of the organization's mission and goals. Developing volunteer positions that relate directly to the organization's mission and building positive relationships between paid and volunteer staff are integral components of a program's success. The degree to which organizational goals are achieved and the advancement of a volunteer administrator's career depend in large part on the administrator's ability to involve volunteers effectively in the accomplishment of an organization's mission.

Plans for staffing are developed in two distinct phases. In the first phase, the organization examines the tasks best performed by volunteer staff in light of its mission, organizational structure, and personnel policies. In the second phase, specific volunteer positions and position guides are developed. Unfortunately, many organizations rush headlong into the second phase. This course neglects the important foundation created in the first phase and leads potentially to conflict between volunteer and paid staff as well as to volunteer assignments that fail to advance organizational goals.

Phase One: Staffing and the Organization's Mission

The first phase in staffing for an organization that has volunteers or is considering involving volunteers is to examine the fundamental motivation for doing so. Is the organization simply looking for free labor in response to budget cuts? Has the organization explored the unique contributions beyond unpaid services that volunteers may make? What philosophical and ethical considerations motivate the decision to involve volunteers? These questions require discussion and resolution prior to the development of specific volunteer positions and activities.

The outcome of such an examination is a formal policy statement that articulates the mission and goals of the organization, describes the role of volunteers in attaining these goals, and defines the nature of the volunteer/paid-staff partnership. After adoption by the organization's board of directors or chief policy-making group, this statement provides a foundation for all staffing decisions within the organization. The involvement and support of the executive director in this process is essential for implementation and maintenance of a volunteer program that reflects the organization's philosophy.

The following case demonstrates how one organization defined and articulated its beliefs:

A large social service agency with a 100-year history of involving volunteers reexamined its philosophy of vol-

unteer involvement and developed a policy statement.
The analysis was initiated by the volunteer administrator in close consultation with the paid managers
of each of the agency's seven different volunteer programs. The effort had the full support of the agency's
executive director as well as the involvement of key
volunteers. The policy statement began with a clear
description of the agency's mission: "The agency,
founded in 1882, shall promote quality family life
through community leadership, family advocacy, innovative counseling, education, and support services to
families in the larger metropolitan community."

The statement continued with a discussion of the agency's philosophy about volunteer services and the role of volunteers in the agency's program:

The agency's volunteer program promotes quality involvement of volunteers in the delivery of agency services to families based on the following beliefs:

1. Volunteers bring unique contributions to the de-
    livery of services to families; areas such as preven-
    tion, education, and support are best served by
    their involvement.
2. Volunteers allow the agency to expand its re-
    sources and reach more families than it could
    with paid staff alone.
3. Volunteers bring a useful community perspective
    to program planning, implementation, and eval-
    uation.
4. Volunteers are strong representatives of the agency
    throughout the community.

No single statement of policy regarding volunteer involvement can apply to all types of organizations. Each must develop a
version that reflects its own values, mission, structure, and goals. It
is essential that the policy statement emphasize the organization's

commitment to volunteer services and describe generally the roles of volunteers and paid staff. Only then does it provide a useful foundation on which the volunteer administrator can design volunteer positions that increase the effectiveness of the organization.

Such a policy statement is necessary in all organizations that involve volunteers, whether those volunteers establish policy and paid staff deliver services or whether paid staff make administrative decisions and volunteers provide direct services. On the basis of such a policy statement, an organization may analyze its present and future services to determine which are most appropriately and effectively delivered by volunteers. Furthermore, it may differentiate the roles that volunteers and paid staff are most capable and motivated to perform in order to establish a complementary relationship between volunteers and paid staff. Volunteer roles may then be developed, based on the unique qualities volunteers bring to program activities and consistent with the organization's philosophy. The AVA offers guidelines for the ethical involvement of volunteers (see Chapter Nine and Resource A). Organizations may find the AVA guidelines useful in the development of a statement of philosophy.

As roles for volunteer staff are explored, persons who are involved in the process are likely to have greater commitment to the resulting plans and decisions than those who are not. Therefore, the participation of board members, union leaders, paid staff, direct-service volunteers, and clients is essential to provide for the broadest possible conceptualization and continuing support of volunteer involvement. Such a cooperative venture provides the opportunity for paid staff and volunteers to work together in the formulation of policy and in the creation of volunteer roles. In this joint effort, volunteers and paid staff may view each other as partners in fulfilling the agency's mission rather than as competitors. Not all paid staff and not all volunteers can be part of the development of such a statement; however, both groups can participate in an annual review and discussion of the statement and can use it as a guide in the formation of new volunteer positions.

The following case study illustrates the relationship between an agency's mission, its philosophy of volunteer/paid-staff relationships, and its decision regarding volunteer involvement in a new service to clients. Observe how the rationale for the use of volunteers is based on the nature of the problem, the program goals, the unique abilities of volunteers, and the interaction between volunteers and paid staff.

> An organization whose mission is the enhancement of the quality of family life noted a significant increase in the number of adolescent mothers in its community. The organization received funding to implement a program that included pre- and postnatal health care, home care services, and educational and counseling services for this population; all these services were to be delivered by paid staff. The goals of the program were to prevent child abuse and neglect, prevent second pregnancies, and assist the adolescent in completing high school and establishing positive life goals.
>
> The organization's board of directors had adopted a policy for involving volunteers in service delivery. It required that volunteers not duplicate the work of paid staff but rather perform tasks for which they were uniquely qualified and that complemented the services of paid staff. In examining ways in which volunteers might help the adolescent mothers, the organization noted that these mothers lacked positive role models who could help them make wise parenting decisions and foster growth in their self-esteem. In response, the organization decided to involve volunteers in a one-to-one relationship with the teen mothers through a separately funded program.
>
> After initiating a relationship with the teen mother with whom she is matched, a volunteer consults with paid staff to set specific goals and design activities. The goals are written down, and the volunteer records observations about client progress toward those goals on a monthly basis. The manager of the volunteer program serves as an ongoing consultant and arranges for continuing education and supervision for the volunteers.

This organization's policy illustrates the close link between an organization's mission, its goals, and its policy of volunteer involvement; the illustration shows how an organization's mission statement affects the design of its volunteer program and influences program development. The role of volunteers is consistent with the organization's philosophy and is clearly differentiated from the role of paid staff. Because the organization's philosophy toward volunteer involvement is a policy of the organization's board of directors, the volunteer administrator was able to develop a volunteer program to respond to a need with complete confidence of organizational support.

Furthermore, the organization's policy affirms the importance of volunteers to its mission. Such strong endorsement of the involvement of volunteers inhibits trivialization of volunteer responsibilities and maintains respect for volunteers as integral members of the organization's staff.

Phase Two: Development of Volunteer Positions

The second phase in the staffing process comprises the design of particular volunteer positions and the development of related position guides. This important step needs to be completed well before recruitment strategies are initiated.

Design of Positions

An approach to the creation of volunteer jobs that balances the needs of clients, paid staff, and volunteers is likely to ensure that each group is satisfied with the staffing decisions. This approach requires a comprehensive understanding of the population to be served by the organization. Questions to be considered include the following:

* What are the characteristics, strengths, and needs of the target population?
* What qualifications will volunteers need in order to serve this population effectively through the program?

- What are the preferences of the target population regarding service delivery by paid staff or volunteers?
- How do the possible volunteer positions relate to the overall mission of the agency?

In the design of volunteer positions Scheier (1980b) strongly advocates that paid staff be involved as well as volunteers and clients. Paid staff are encouraged to list the tasks they would rather not do ("spinoffs") and the activities they wish they could do but cannot ("dreams"). Then, the volunteer administrator, at least one current or potential volunteer, and representatives of the paid staff integrate the tasks and activities listed to create meaningful volunteer jobs. The volunteer administrator monitors the process to ensure that volunteer roles are developed in a manner consistent with the organization's philosophy of volunteerism and the ethical guidelines suggested by the AVA. An important outcome of Scheier's process is that when paid staff have a voice and investment in the design of volunteer positions, they are likely to view volunteer involvement as a positive element and be committed to working in partnership with volunteer staff.

Scheier's (1980b, p. 16) process is also sensitive to the need for volunteer positions to be highly attractive. Volunteers are not asked simply to do those tasks that paid staff members dislike. Instead, routine tasks are combined with more interesting activities in order to create a "purposeful and unified whole." As in any paid or unpaid position, not all the individual tasks will be attractive or inspiring, but a position will be attractive when it includes a sufficient number of meaningful and desirable activities clearly related to the organization's mission. The whole volunteer job is greater than the sum of its parts.

Wilson (1976) points out that the principal satisfaction volunteers receive is from the work they do. Each job is its own reward and must offer a gratifying experience. This suggestion contrasts with current views of work, which have been strongly influenced by that epitome of efficiency, the assembly line. Work is fragmented into many small, specialized components with little concern for the satisfaction of the worker. Drucker's (1974, p. 411) advice that "a job should be specific enough so that a man can go to work and do it, but so big that he can't get his arms around it" also encourages the development of volunteer positions that provide an interesting combination of tasks and opportunities for valuable service, achievement, and personal growth.

Position Guides

Although a volunteer position is commonly described in a job description or work assignment, the term *position guide* is more appropriate; it implies flexibility and sensitivity to the needs and interests of volunteers. It also distinguishes volunteer efforts from paid-staff jobs. The following illustration underlines the importance of position guides for volunteer positions and describes how they benefit staff, volunteers, clients, and others with whom volunteers interact.

> A social service agency was collaborating with a day-care center to deliver an intensive thirteen-week educational program for a group of families who were clients of both organizations. Three volunteers from the social service agency cofacilitated the program. The day-care center decided it would offer a dinner for the families prior to the start of each weekly session. At the end of the first evening, the paid staff from the day-care center asked the three volunteers to stay and help clean up after the dinner.
>
> The next day, the volunteers called their program manager to complain about the situation. They had helped clean up but did not want to do so for the remaining twelve weeks; furthermore, they had not realized it was part of their assignment.
>
> The volunteer administrator promptly replied that cleanup was definitely not part of the original position guide nor was it what the volunteers had been prepared to do in the thirty hours of training they had completed in order to be accepted as facilitators for the series. She called the day-care center, reviewed the contents of the volunteer position guide

with a paid staff member, and notified him that other paid or volunteer staff would need to be found to handle cleanup in the coming weeks.

The volunteer administrator learned that in the future she had to make certain that staff at collaborating agencies had expectations of the volunteers that matched their position guides. She also learned that she needed to make volunteers aware of their own rights so that they could respond to inappropriate requests based on knowledge of the guides.

Position guides describe the responsibilities of the position, the qualifications needed by prospective volunteers, the system of supervision and accountability, and the means of measuring successful performance. Each position guide also includes a title for the position and a statement of the degree of commitment expected—both length of appointment and amount of time. In addition, benefits of volunteering are an important part of the position guide. Well-developed position guides that clarify how each staff position contributes to the attainment of organizational goals aid in avoiding confusion over expectations and maximize retention of both volunteers and paid staff.

To prepare a guide for a position in which volunteers are currently functioning, incumbent volunteers may be asked to describe all the activities for which they are responsible and any benefits they receive from volunteering. In organizations where jobs are being reorganized or new positions are being added, the core of the position guides is usually a task analysis in which all the discrete activities that are to be part of a particular position are listed. Qualifications, commitment, and accountability then depend on the activities listed.

Effective design of positions for volunteers, according to Lynch (1983), includes four key elements. The first element is to provide the volunteer with a sense of "turf." Lynch found that volunteers who do one task repeatedly (such as stuffing envelopes) get less satisfaction than volunteers who perform several tasks (collating, stapling, folding, stuffing, stamping, and sorting). The second key element is to ensure that the volunteer has the opportunity and authority to think about as well as perform the job. Thinking includes planning, organizing, deciding, and evaluating. Standard management practice typically finds the supervisor doing the planning, organizing, and deciding, and the employee carrying out the plan. This practice may work best for some paid staff and may be necessary for new volunteers. However, experienced volunteers will likely desire involvement in the planning process and will have a contribution to make to it. To improve the design of positions, Wilson (1976) too suggests job enlargement, increasing the number and variety of tasks; job enrichment, increasing responsibility to include planning and evaluating the work for which the volunteer is responsible; and work simplification, eliminating trivial tasks and combining others. Increased ownership results from participation in both the planning and the implementation of an activity, and it provides increased satisfaction with the volunteer activity.

Lynch's third element of program design is to assure that position guides communicate responsibility for achieving results linked directly to the agency's mission and goals, rather than simply for performing a list of activities. Having responsibility for results focuses attention on the outcomes of the activity rather than on the activity itself, thereby encouraging volunteers to be motivated by their accomplishments. The fourth element deals with the measurement of performance and results. With a clear understanding of how to measure the success of an effort and one's participation in it, the volunteer will be able to assess the value of his or her own contributions. Additionally, the volunteer administrator will have a tool to use in discussions with volunteers regarding any needed improvements in their performance.

Occasionally volunteers may find that they cannot discharge the responsibilities outlined in the position guide. It may then be necessary to renegotiate the position guide on an individual basis. Scheier (1980b) cautions that inflexibility in volunteer position guides may preclude valuable volunteers from becoming involved; he suggests that parts of position guides be sufficiently flexible to permit volunteer administrators to modify them depending on the interests, preferences, and capabilities of the volunteer. These variations may include task performance by individuals or groups, on a regular or occasional basis, in person or at a distance, in a direct-service or advisory capacity, or through a formal or informal relationship.

Position guides vary in specificity. Volunteer positions relating to policy-making, such as membership on a board of directors, or to a major responsibility of the organization, such as directing a fundraising campaign, are usually described according to broad areas of responsibility. Guides for positions that provide direct services tend to be much more specific in listing duties and time requirements. Marx (1981) advocates listing the major tasks in each area as one way to increase specificity.

Failure to provide well-developed position guides may result in confusion, misunderstanding, personnel problems, and ineffective management. Consider the following illustration:

> Teen volunteers at a hands-on children's museum were serving as exhibit aides. Some teens stood passively near their assigned exhibit and answered questions only when a visitor spoke to them first, uncertain whether to initiate activities and unsure of how to do so. Adult volunteers who served in the same position spoke to the volunteer administrator about the performance of the teens. She responded by revising their position guide to be more specific.
>
> She involved both adult and teen volunteers in developing a list of specific actions that outlined step-by-step the kind of performance expected of all exhibit monitors. These actions included making eye contact with all visitors, greeting all visitors with a smile, encouraging visitors to touch or do whatever the particular exhibit offered, and modeling how to use the exhibit for inhibited or confused visitors. These actions had all been encouraged during the volunteer training program but had not been presented in list form as performance criteria. Both teen and adult volunteers improved their performance as a result.

Many similar direct-service positions need to be described by using a behavioral approach to listing responsibilities required of the volunteer.

Sample Position Guide

The following guide is typical for a volunteer position that provides a direct service to clients. The headings used for the various components can serve as a format for position guides in almost any type of organization.

Job Title:	Family Friend
Program Goal:	To prevent child abuse and provide the opportunity for a more positive future for children and parents by assisting in the social and educational development of a teen-parent family.
Objectives:	• Develop a nurturing relationship with a single, adolescent mother.
	• Build on the mother's strengths.
	• Facilitate her personal growth and development.
	• Increase her competence and self-esteem.
	• Encourage her to become a positive role model for her children.
	• Promote healthy parenting.
Responsibilities:	Visit with the assigned client for a minimum of two hours per week. Set goals in consultation with the client's social worker and chart client progress on a weekly basis. Participate in a regular monthly supervision group with other vol-

unteers and the program manager. Seek individual consultation with the program manager or social worker or both as needed.

Qualifications:
- At least twenty-one years of age.
- Mobile.
- Skilled in relating to a variety of racial groups and accepting persons from various cultural traditions.
- Able to observe and report concerns about client progress to the program manager, operating independently and with good judgment.
- Experienced as a parent.

Training and Supervision: A nine-hour orientation to the agency and the program is provided, along with ongoing, monthly continuing education on topics such as family and individual development, needs of the target population, dynamics of child abuse, communication skills. Two regularly scheduled supervision meetings are provided per month. Individual consultation is available on an as-needed basis.

Evaluation: Formal evaluation of the volunteer/client relationship and client progress toward goals occurs after three months, after six months, and annually. A performance review is offered as part of the exit interview.

Commitment: Volunteers are required to commit

two to three hours per week for a minimum of one year. After one year, the assignment may end and the volunteer may choose to continue with the same client, may take on a new client, or may decide to leave the program.

Benefits:
- Opportunity for the personal growth that results from serving as a caring friend and role model to an adolescent mother.
- Opportunity to increase interpersonal skills from working closely with social work staff with master's degrees and to receive continuing education on the dynamics of teen parenting, child-abuse prevention, and high-risk populations.
- Position-related expenses are reimbursed up to $40 per month.

This position guide contains specific information about the goal of the program, the objectives to be achieved, the responsibilities to be assumed by the volunteer, and the manner in which work is to be evaluated. The qualifications and the level of commitment expected of the volunteer are also clearly stated. Expressions of the organization's commitment to the volunteer—through the provision of training, supervision, and benefits—are also included in the position guide. Notice how the four key elements described by Lynch (1983)—sense of turf, opportunity to think about as well as do the job, orientation toward job outcomes, and clear standards for measuring performance—are included in the position guide.

The use of position guides that explicitly describe the tasks in which the volunteer will be engaged and the expectations regarding the results to be achieved has a positive impact on volunteers. They see that the organization values their work and approaches it as seriously as that of paid staff. And when volunteer roles stress achievement of outcomes, the impact of all the activities of volunteers on the organization's mission may be assessed and appreciated. When volunteer roles are described so as to avoid disagreement over responsibilities, paid-staff/volunteer relationships are off to a promising start.

An Overall Approach to Job Design

Volunteer administrators, like most management professionals, work through other persons to attain organizational goals. Their ability to lead and manage volunteer personnel is critical for the achievement of those goals. Likert (1961) wrote that management will make full use of its human resources only when each person in the organization is a member of one or more effectively functioning work groups that have a high degree of group loyalty, good interaction skills, and high performance goals. The volunteer administrator's role is to plan and lead in this process and to lay the groundwork for positive working relationships between volunteers and paid staff.

Drucker (1974, p. 307), in asserting that the function of managing in an organization is "to make the strengths of people productive and their weaknesses irrelevant," suggests a helpful overall approach to staffing decisions that will increase both the effectiveness of volunteer staff and the ability of the organization to integrate volunteers and paid personnel. A hierarchical approach emphasizes control, accountability, and efficiency among superiors and subordinates and often fails to accomplish the integration of paid staff and volunteers. In contrast, a team approach emphasizes the participation of all personnel in decision making. When this approach is applied to volunteer administration, worker ownership and commitment are enhanced, relations between paid and volunteer staff are improved, and increased cooperation and productivity may be expected.

Conclusion

Staffing considerations are addressed on both the organizational and program-management levels. At the organizational level, sound staffing decisions are based on the mission and goals of the organization, the organization's philosophy about involving volunteers, and the relationship between volunteers and paid staff. At the program level, sound staffing decisions are based on the design of meaningful volunteer positions and comprehensive position guides. Good staffing decisions are the foundation of a well-developed volunteer program and enable volunteers to make a difference in the life of the organization and in the lives of those it is designed to serve.

Volunteerism as an expression of caring for one's neighbor has been an integral part of human history. Increasing needs to organize volunteers to solve community problems, finance programs, and provide a broad range of needed services to all segments of society, combined with decreasing amounts of time available from volunteers, have required that managers of volunteer programs understand and use many of the management principles previously associated with business (Henderson, 1983). When properly adapted for volunteer programs, basic management tools such as written mission statements and position guides are applicable. Although volunteer staff have characteristics that distinguish them from paid employees, both groups are organized to engage in regular purposeful activities and require equally skilled management.

3

Building a Volunteer Staff: A Systematic Approach

The professional volunteer administrator recognizes that selection of volunteer staff can and should involve the same careful procedures used for hiring paid personnel. The challenge to the volunteer administrator is to devise and implement a process that is not so formal as to discourage qualified volunteers and yet not so informal as to suggest that any candidate who applies will be accepted. McCurley and Lynch (1989) promote the concept of the selection process as a negotiation, one in which compromises will result in mutual agreement between the prospective volunteer and the organization. When selection is designed as a mutual process, the needs of both the volunteer and the organization can be met, and volunteer performance will likely be effective. As a comfortable balance is reached, candidates for positions feel a warm and open reception by the organization and, at the same time, are helped to understand the organization's need for a thoughtful and deliberate volunteer-selection process.

Specific Inquiries for Jobs

We discuss first the selection process for prospective volunteers who inquire about particular positions they have reason to believe are open within an organization. These individuals have heard about the organization and the volunteer position (through a newspaper story, recruitment brochure, volunteer center, posting at work, or word of mouth), have a preliminary sense of the requirements, and feel comfortable enough about their qualifications to make an initial inquiry. They contact the organization to express interest and to learn how to become involved.

Volunteer administrators can achieve success in identifying the best candidates for positions in these circumstances if they devise a systematic approach that includes the following components: a task and qualifications analysis, an application form, a personal interview, and a screening mechanism. Volunteer administrators can develop a sequence for these components to suit their own styles and situations.

Task and Qualifications Analysis

The most basic and the most important information personnel administrators possess is a good description of the positions that need to be filled. Volunteer administrators require detailed information about vacant positions, which includes specifics about the work load, time requirements, number of volunteer staff needed, tasks to be performed, and necessary qualifications. All well-developed volunteer position guides include this detailed information.

The tasks to be performed and the qualifications needed by staff are closely linked. Examination of the tasks involved in a position typically makes the general qualifications required for effective performance readily apparent. The challenge to the volunteer administrator is to further define specific qualifications so that the right candidate for the position also becomes as apparent. (See Chapter Two for additional information on position guides and task analysis.)

One way to approach qualifications analysis is by examining position guides for information about the knowledge, skills, and abilities required for success (Prien and Schippman, 1987, p. 63):

> *Knowledge* is defined as an organized body of key information which makes adequate performance of the job possible and is the foundation upon which abilities and skills are built. Possession of knowledge, however, does not ensure its proper application. A

volunteer may possess the required knowledge but still lack the ability to apply that knowledge due to lack of self-confidence, lack of understanding of the cultural group to be served, lack of personal commitment to the cause, and lack of time.

Skill is the proficient manual, verbal, or mental manipulation of people, ideas, or things. A skill is demonstrable. Skills differ from abilities in that possession of a skill implies a performance standard to be met. Willingness or enthusiasm does not always bring with it adequate skill levels. Therefore, a minimal skill level must be defined along with a method of assessing each applicant's proficiency.

Ability is the power to perform a job function, to complete the activity while applying or using the essential knowledge. Power to perform the job may be impaired by such things as time availability, attitude, and motivation. An individual can have both the knowledge and skill required to complete a task, yet be unable to do so.

An additional measure that may be the key element to successful performance is a subjective category best described as fit. In a good fit the volunteer's beliefs and values parallel the organization's mission and philosophy, and the volunteer's personality is compatible with those of current paid and volunteer staff. Determination of fit requires judgment on the part of the volunteer administrator who must combine an objective assessment of knowledge, skill, and ability with a subjective look at the personal elements the individual may bring to the position.

Broad descriptions of qualifications such as "the ability to work with people" are generally not useful in the selection process unless further defined by specific characteristics or skills. For example, "the ability to work with people" may, in one position, require a nonjudgmental attitude toward races and cultures different from one's own. In another position, it may require skill in consensus building and group decision making. When volunteer administrators have identified the precise qualifications needed for a particular volunteer role, they have a strong base from which to implement the staff-selection process.

Once task analysis is completed and a list of qualifications is developed, the volunteer administrator needs to consult with other staff to determine which areas of knowledge, which skills, and which abilities potential volunteers must bring with them in order to be selected and which of these the organization will develop through training. If training will be provided, the organization may waive a particular qualification subject to volunteers' successfully completing a program designed to equip them with the knowledge, skills, or abilities they may not currently possess.

Whatever decision is made by an organization regarding its willingness and capacity to provide volunteers with training, task and qualifications analysis prepares a foundation on which to examine the work history, life experiences, and personal characteristics of candidates in order to assess the likelihood of their success in particular volunteer positions.

Application Form

The application form is an essential component in the selection process. If it is well designed, it can significantly increase the efficiency of the selection process. An application enables the volunteer administrator to make a preliminary assessment of the qualifications of candidates without conducting time-consuming interviews of all prospective volunteers. A well-developed application form has a professional appearance and includes the name, address, phone number, and logo of the organization. Although each form will be custom-designed to fit the needs of the organization, the following categories of information are normally included: applicant's name, address, work and home phone numbers, whether the applicant can be contacted at the work phone number, occupation, current or most recent employer, employer's address and phone number, education, and any special training. Commonly asked questions pertain to the applicant's current or past volunteer experiences, personal goals that may relate to the volunteer position, ability to give the time needed and to meet other expectations, qualifications for the position, and how the applicant became aware of the organization and the position. A request for two or three personal or professional references is common. The completed application form becomes the first item kept in each prospective volunteer's file.

The information gained through task and qualifications analysis suggests the information to be solicited from candidates on the application form. For example, if the tasks require evening or weekend hours, the application form can seek information about availability during those hours. If qualifications include a minimum age level or the ability to drive an automobile, the form can be used to gather this information. When designed this way, the form can gather specific job-relevant information for use by the volunteer administrator.

Personal Interview

Another important step in the selection process is the interview. McCurley and Lynch (1989) suggest that the interview belongs to the volunteer as much as it does to the organization. They see the process as one of mutual exchange in which the volunteer has an opportunity to express concerns, ask questions, and gain information, and the organization has an opportunity to "sell" the volunteer position while at the same time assessing the suitability of the candidate. Macduff (1985) suggests that the interview have a double focus: what the organization needs to know about the volunteer in order to assess the possibility of a placement and what the volunteer needs to know about the organization and the position in order to determine whether to make a commitment.

An interview structured around a particular job provides the most accurate and comprehensive information about each candidate. If the prospective volunteer has completed an application form prior to the interview, the interviewer can focus on what is not known about the candidate that pertains to the job. The interviewer may want to note key questions that remain after a review of the candidate's responses on the application form so that these items are addressed.

There is no neat formula for interviewing candidates, but volunteer administrators may find the following guidelines helpful:

1. Let the candidate know what to expect during the interview and why certain facts or responses to questions are needed. Make sure the candidate knows the interviewer's position and role in the organization.
2. Create a nonthreatening, friendly yet professional atmosphere; do not take phone calls or allow other unnecessary interruptions. Give full attention to the candidate. Arrange seating so it is comfortable and encourages conversation. Because this is a private interview, conduct it in a private office. Establish a rapport with the candidate conducive to the sharing of feelings, preferences, strengths, and weaknesses.
3. Be organized. Refer to the candidate's completed application form (if one has been filled out prior to the interview) as well as other materials needed to conduct the interview.
4. Follow the same basic interview format with all candidates. When similar questions are asked, all candidates have an equal chance to present their qualifications. Explore their responses with further questions or related observations.
5. Set the candidate at ease; let each one know the interview is not a test but rather a way to discover whether the volunteer position suits the needs and interests of both parties.
6. Let the candidate do most of the talking!
7. Subtly direct the flow of the conversation with simple questions such as "Can you tell me more about that?" or "What else do you feel is important for me to know?" or "Can you give me another example?"
8. Close the interview by allowing the candidate to ask any remaining questions and informing the candidate of the next step in the selection process.

According to Wilson (1976, p. 122), the interview will "have a greater impact on the quality of our programs in years to come than any other single factor, for it will determine which people will be involved in designing, directing and carrying out those programs." For this reason, one interview is not sufficient. After an initial interview with the volunteer administrator, the best candidates for a position commonly participate in a second interview with both the volunteer administrator and the staff person who will supervise the volunteer. This procedure involves the supervisor in the selection process in a meaningful way and facilitates the formation of positive volunteer/staff relations.

Risk Management

Tremper (1989, p. 138) defines risk management as a method to identify potential negative situations and to implement appropriate measures to prevent them. The screening of volunteer staff is an essential component of a nonprofit organization's risk-management plan and one of the most critical jobs of the volunteer administrator.

Volunteer administrators most often associate the term *screening* with the process of identifying unsuitable or inappropriate candidates for volunteer positions. However, in its broadest sense, screening applies to the positive identification of qualified candidates as well. The entire process of comparing the experience, skills, and personal characteristics of candidates with the qualifications required can be considered a form of screening. Thus, prospective volunteers can be screened in as well as out. This section, however, will focus on techniques for screening out inappropriate volunteers through the development and implementation of effective risk-management measures.

Screening is an essential and often delicate part of the selection process, particularly for organizations serving vulnerable populations such as children, the frail elderly, and the disabled. I. H. Scheier (cited in Wilson, 1976, p. 122) offers the following reasons for screening out individuals who are clearly unsuited for certain jobs:

- The clients of the organization must be protected. They must be helped, not hindered, by any volunteer involvement.
- The organization's reputation is greatly affected by the volunteers who work there.
- Morale of paid staff and other volunteers declines when inappropriate or poor volunteer placements occur.
- The volunteer suffers when misplaced.

A barrier at times encountered in risk management is concern on the part of volunteer administrators that too aggressive screening of volunteers might cause good candidates to lose interest or withdraw their applications because they perceive distrust on the part of the organization or an invasion of privacy. Although unfortunate, when weighed against the chance that vulnerable clients may be at risk from a volunteer with unsuitable motivations or a criminal background, the loss is worth taking. If the organization's screening process is communicated with empathy, clarity, sensitivity, and understanding, volunteer allegiance, performance, and commitment can be significantly enhanced.

Newmann and Montgomery (1989) suggest that the most effective screening techniques are uniquely designed to match the specific situation and volunteer/client relationship. For a program serving children, they recommend that volunteer administrators learn the key characteristics and behaviors of child molesters and incorporate this knowledge into the design of interview questions and observation of candidates in a variety of situations, such as a group orientation session, a discussion about the needs of children, and training sessions that include role-play activities. They also encourage the use of criminal-record checks as the primary risk-management technique in all programs that match volunteers one-to-one with vulnerable clients.

Additionally, Newmann and Montgomery recommend that screening not stop once a criminal-record check is conducted or once an interview is completed and the volunteer is placed in a position. Rather, the volunteer administrator should deliberately use supervision sessions, the volunteer's written reports on interaction with the client, and client evaluation of the volunteer as ongoing risk-management measures. Although the primary objective of these measures is to help the volunteer administrator or supervisor recognize patterns of behavior that disqualify a person for the volunteer position, they can also be a source of positive feedback to volunteers who are providing quality service to clients.

An organization that has developed effective screening mechanisms unique to its situation is the American Field Service (AFS). The American Field Service Center for the Study of Intercultural Learning (1984) conducted numerous studies over a twenty-five-year period to develop criteria for selecting candidates for AFS international study experiences. They identified nine personal qualities that research showed to be especially valuable in enabling people to meet the challenges of extended intercultural living. Guidelines on what to ask and what to look for regarding each of the nine qualities were developed and are used by search-and-screen committees to select candidates for participation in their program. AFS recommends that information on candidates come from a wide variety of sources: personal interviews, family members, peers, and observations of candidates in various situations (social functions, simulation games, group discussions).

Clearly, risk-management issues vary with each situation depending on the nature of the volunteer role. The volunteer administrator may want to seek the advice of legal counsel to determine which forms of screening are necessary for particular volunteer positions. The following are four of the options available.

First, the volunteer application form can be designed to serve as a self-screening device. Certain questions on the form can stimulate self-assessment by volunteers regarding their qualifications. A question such as "What kind of prior training and/or experience do you feel is needed to be effective in this position?" may serve as a self-screening tool for some candidates. Responses to this question will also provide the volunteer administrator with a sense of the prospective volunteer's grasp of the knowledge, skills, and abilities needed in the position.

Second, the application form may include an attitudinal survey that can be used to assess whether the candidate's personal philosophy and beliefs are compatible with those of the organization. This is not to suggest that organizations serve themselves best by attempting to recruit staff who share completely the same attitudes and beliefs. However, it is important to discover attitudes and beliefs that may be totally inappropriate for the position or in conflict with those held by the organization. For example, an organization that had developed a policy statement forbidding all forms of physical punishment of children asked candidates for child-care positions about their child-management practices and beliefs. A volunteer administrator for a mentoring program for adolescent mothers asked volunteers to respond to a statement about the socialization needs of teen parents.

Third, a commonly used screening tool is the personal or professional reference. The volunteer application form typically includes a space for the names, addresses, and telephone numbers of several references. Macduff (1987) recommends that the same set of questions be used in each reference check made. References can be contacted by telephone or mail. If references are contacted by mail, a cover letter should be included that provides an overview of the position and the qualifications needed. A stamped, preaddressed envelope should also be provided. If contact is made by telephone, the same introductory information should be provided. Questions depend on the needs of a specific position; however, they commonly focus on the capacity in which the reference has known the applicant, an assessment of the applicant's reliability and judgment, and the personal qualities that will enable the applicant to perform well in the volunteer position.

Fourth, volunteers can be asked to sign a statement saying that they have full knowledge that a check on their criminal record is part of the agency's screening process and that they give full permission for the investigation. The program manager then simply contacts the police department and a computerized record search takes place based on the volunteer's name, birth date, and race. Informing prospective volunteers about the record check may deter some with a criminal record from continuing with their application. Other applicants, when informed of the screening process, may share information with the interviewer about past arrests. If the nature of the arrests lack relevance to the volunteer position, the volunteers need not be denied an opportunity to be part of the program. However, when persons refuse to give permission for the criminal-record check, they are not accepted as volunteers in the program.

General Inquiries for Jobs

Some individuals contact an organization to express interest in volunteering in general rather than in response to particular position openings. A volunteer administrator at a counseling center frequently received such inquiries and designed the following selection process to handle them.

The first phase, getting acquainted, begins when a potential volunteer contacts the organization and a personal interview with the volunteer administrator is scheduled. Immediately following the interview, the candidate views a slide presentation that provides a general introduction to the organization. Included is information on its history, mission, funding, current programs, important policies, structure, philosophy, and volunteer opportunities. The candidate then tours the facility, which allows the volunteer administrator to review and reinforce information included in the slide presentation and to introduce the potential volunteer to the staff and setting in which the volunteer will work. The tour ends in the office of the volunteer administrator and is followed by discussion of whether there may be a place for the individual within the organization.

If in the opinion of the volunteer administrator there is no suitable opening for the candidate, the volunteer administrator explains the situation and may make a referral to another nonprofit organization where the candidate's skills may be used. If, however, the volunteer administrator feels there is a suitable position for the candidate, information on that position is presented at this time. The administrator describes general duties, responsibilities, time commitment, and growth opportunities in detail. The administrator also encourages the individual to seriously consider becoming part of the organization and presents the candidate with literature about the organization and an application form. At the end of the interview, the volunteer administrator explains that the next step in the application process is an interview with the supervisor of the volunteer position. The first phase concludes when the administrator writes a short summary of the interview, which becomes part of the volunteer's permanent file.

The second phase, assessment, begins when the candidate returns a completed application form. The volunteer administrator then meets with the appropriate supervisor to review the application and interview summary and to discuss initial impressions and any concerns about the qualifications of the applicant. The supervisor and volunteer administrator review the written job description to assess whether the applicant's skills, education, and time availability meet the requirements of the position. When necessary, the volunteer administrator offers suggestions for job modifications that may be required to accommodate the volunteer. At this time, a decision is made to accept the candidate into the program or to recommend another type of volunteer position.

Short-Term Volunteers

Scheier (1980a) refers to "occasional" volunteers who are involved in the organization on a less frequent, less organized basis than regular volunteers. The use of such volunteers is a rising trend. Their jobs can range from helping annually with some aspect of a fundraiser to playing the piano for a holiday party at a nursing home to contacting the volunteer administrator with information related to the program or the organization's services in general. A volunteer administrator may also contact an occasional volunteer for advice on a specific issue on which the volunteer is known to be an expert. Macduff (1990) uses the term *episodic* to describe short-term volunteers. She suggests that if organizations recognize and design their programs to include this type of volunteer, they can tap a beneficial resource.

Do episodic volunteer positions require the same careful selection procedures as those filled in more traditional ways? Is such a selection process practical or necessary? The answer lies in the responsibilities involved. The following situation requires an abbreviated form of selection:

> A volunteer center maintains a list of individuals with special skills (often known as a skills bank); the list can be used by any nonprofit organization in the community. A volunteer administrator using this service to locate an individual to do calligraphy occasionally for recognition certificates is not likely to spend a great deal of time interviewing and screening candidates. A sample of the volunteer's work and a verbal agreement regarding the volunteer's ability to complete the project by a certain date are probably all that is necessary in this case.

Volunteer administrators are often charged with finding volunteers for large-scale fundraisers or special events such as telethons, walkathons, Special Olympics, or church fairs. Qualifications, time commitments, and degree of responsibility for these positions vary significantly. Volunteer administrators select the chairs for such events and the committee chairs with much more care and attention to qualifications than they invest in the selection of volunteers who register participants, make posters, serve food, sell tickets, direct traffic, or perform other less complicated tasks.

Group projects also require a modified version of the selection process. Many companies have programs that involve groups of employees in volunteer projects; these projects can vary from a one-time activity to a short- or long-term commitment. They range from painting a disabled person's house to organizing a Christmas party for disadvantaged children to selling hot dogs and candy at a fundraiser concession stand.

A volunteer administrator cannot afford to invest great amounts of time interviewing and screening prospective volunteers for occasional responsibilities. However, a number of procedures can be followed to ensure the appropriateness and reliability of these individuals:

- Written guidelines for task performance can be prepared by the volunteer administrator and distributed prior to the activity.
- The volunteer administrator can provide an orientation session prior to the activity.
- The volunteer administrator can arrange for training for lead volunteers who then offer on-the-job training and supervision to their coworkers on the day of the event.

Volunteers in Membership Organizations

Many opportunities for volunteer involvement occur through organizations such as churches, parent-teacher organizations, community-improvement and professional associations, where volunteer positions are filled by members of the organization.

The advantage here is having a pool of persons who have indicated some interest in the organization's mission. Members are usually acquainted with the organization's structure and functions and share its purpose; often they require minimal orientation to the organization and the position. Membership in the organization may already represent a commitment to a cause that needs only to be channeled in a particular and specific responsibility.

Organizations often gather information about the interests and skills of members periodically in order to place them in suitable volunteer positions. Because members of organizations have continuing personal and social relationships, informal information is also available about the talents and needs of individual volunteers. Membership organizations typically enjoy great flexibility in their ability to combine tasks to fit the particular talents and schedules of their members.

At the same time, membership groups are frequently constrained by their inability to select volunteers from beyond their own membership. Securing new volunteers for responsibilities within a membership organization often becomes a two-step process: potential volunteers must first be recruited into membership in the organization and later selected for a particular volunteer position or responsibility.

Given the informality and high level of group cohesiveness often found in membership organizations, the maintenance of sound personnel practices is both important and difficult. Because members tend to know the business and functions of the organization, particularly if it is small, practices such as the use of position guides, the use of recognized selection procedures, and the provision of formal training programs are often considered superfluous and are frequently omitted. Lack of variety in available positions may oblige members to fill volunteer jobs when they lack interest or have filled those jobs for several years, making selection difficult. The use of procedures to ensure variety in volunteer options is required to respond to the diverse needs of an organization's members. Moreover, sound selection practices are required to prevent personnel issues from becoming personal.

Legal Considerations

In general, volunteer staff should be selected by using the same nondiscriminatory practices that apply to the hiring of paid staff.

Selection of volunteers should be free of any feature that leads to unequal treatment of applicants. Thus, the application form and personal interview should not include questions regarding marital status, occupation of applicant's spouse, race, gender, national origin, or age. Interviewers rarely have a legitimate need to ask such questions.

Although many organizations have volunteer positions that can be filled appropriately by individuals regardless of age (such as family volunteering, which includes children in activities, or teen and college-student volunteering), some volunteer responsibilities may require that volunteers have legal adult status. In these cases, however, asking candidates for their age is unnecessary if the application form states a minimum age for participation.

Arthur (1986, pp. 77–78) offers the following guidelines for the recording of interview results so that the notes are consistent with equal-opportunity regulations:

- Develop written notes in an objective rather than a subjective manner. The following illustrates the kind of subjective language that should be avoided: pretty, too old, know-it-all, no sense of humor, needs polish.
- Use caution in writing opinions which are not supported by anything factual. "As I see it, Ms. Jones is just right for this position," is a broad statement which does not indicate what qualities and skills make the candidate suitable for the job. Instead, use a statement such as, "Ms. Jones has two years of experience using the same computer program we will be using for this project."
- Use only job-related facts derived from the position guide. . . .
- Record direct quotes from candidates regarding their skill level, motivations for the position, and attitudes. "Mr. Wilson shared that he 'wants to be a mentor for a fatherless young man because he was helped by someone special when his father left the family when he was a teenager.'"

Although most volunteer administrators are not expected to be fully versed in the technical and complex details of personnel law, they are expected to be familiar with general prohibitions such as those listed above and are responsible for conducting their volunteer-selection process fairly. Organizations may wish to seek the advice of a professional in personnel administration to assess the extent to which their current practices comply with hiring regulations.

Conclusion

Selection is a multifaceted process and one of the most important responsibilities of the professional volunteer administrator. The identification of the best candidate for positions is a key to an organization's attainment of its goals. Selection of the best candidate depends on the volunteer administrator's knowledge of the position to be filled, interviewing skills, and ability to match volunteer interests and needs to the opportunities available. The inclusion of other key staff in the selection of volunteer personnel is essential to positive staff/volunteer relationships.

It is critical that volunteer administrators acquire competence in the development and implementation of risk-management techniques. They must also have a basic understanding of legal issues involved in the selection process and develop interview forms and procedures accordingly. Once a systematic approach to selecting volunteers has been developed, the volunteer administrator can begin to plan for recruitment.

4

Establishing an Organizational Climate That Enhances Motivation, Recognition, and Retention

A major task in organizations that involve volunteers in their work is planning for effective recruitment and retention. Enlisting new volunteers, providing them with the skills necessary to undertake their assigned tasks, enhancing their usefulness, and maintaining their continued involvement and loyalty to the organization over a period of time make up the foundation on which successful volunteer programs are built. A program that effectively attracts and retains volunteers prevents great numbers from entering and exiting through a revolving door, saves leaders of volunteer programs from the continual task of replacing them, and provides volunteers with rewarding and lasting experiences, thereby avoiding the following situation.

> A national professional organization has a membership of approximately three thousand, the minimum required to underwrite its program and to support its staff at the present size. A decline in membership, no matter how small, has immediate negative consequences for the services this organization is able to provide to and on behalf of its members. Unfortunately, approximately 25 percent of its members fail to renew each year, thereby forcing the organization's leaders and staff to make the replacement of members their first priority. Studies reveal that although some

of these nonrenewing members move on to other pursuits, many are disappointed in the services they receive, particularly in the organization's failure to involve them expeditiously in volunteer opportunities.

Whether in a national professional association, in a local church or social service organization, or in the volunteer corps of a hospital, recruitment and retention are key issues. They both require an understanding of the motives of volunteers. What prompts individuals to provide services without remuneration, for only some combination of intrinsic and extrinsic rewards? What keeps them performing tasks over time in a dependable, loyal, and effective manner? What provides them with the incentive to undertake new challenges, to increase their area of responsibility, and thereby to add measurably to their contribution to the organization's mission and to their value within the organization?

An analysis of the factors that motivate volunteers is echoed in the awareness of volunteers that there is a magnetism in volunteering that causes a volunteer job to hold their attention, draw their energy, and make them feel rewarded for their involvement. Or, conversely, volunteers may be aware that the magic of volunteering is gone; the job no longer lives up to expectations; loyalty to the task, the organization, or the cause has waned; and other interests are replacing the one at hand. An ex-volunteer once said, "I got to the stage where I decided to stop. If you're doing volunteer work, enthusiasm takes the place of money, and when you run out of enthusiasm, you stop" (Sherrott, 1983, p. 79).

To understand motivation is to be able to anticipate human behavior in particular circumstances and to devise conditions that influence that behavior. The motivation of volunteers and the ways in which organizations and administrators may influence it in the beginning and later stages of the volunteer experience are the subject of this chapter.

Why Volunteer?

Many theories have been developed to aid our understanding of what motivates individuals to behave in specific ways; these theories are supported by the experiences of volunteer administrators. This discussion of how particular theories of motivation contribute to an understanding of volunteer behavior divides motivators into three categories—needs, reasons, and benefits. The first group of theories assumes that individual behavior is a result of internal needs, the second that individuals have conscious reasons for their behavior, and the third that behavior is prompted by expected benefits or rewards.

Needs

Psychological needs influence individuals to participate in volunteer activities. In what has become a classic theory, Maslow (1970) described motivation as the individual's response to internal needs and created a pyramid consisting of physiological, security, socialization, self-esteem, and self-actualization needs. Maslow believed that each of these needs prompts an individual to act in a certain way until that need is met, after which it no longer serves to motivate, and movement to the next higher level of the pyramid occurs. For example, a person would not likely be motivated by social needs until physiological and safety needs were satisfied.

This theory suggests that organizations wishing to attract and retain volunteers need to be sensitive to the needs that are dominant among those they seek. For example, to attract volunteers from disadvantaged groups, an organization frequently must clearly describe how volunteer positions will assist in the satisfaction of physiological and safety needs. Furnishing stipends, transportation, and child care to volunteers is a common way to fulfill physiological needs; however, these incentives have little attraction to volunteers whose needs are for socialization, self-esteem, or self-actualization. Recruitment of volunteers from diverse groups requires a sensitivity to their dominant needs and a presentation of the volunteer experience in ways that indicate how those needs will be met.

Others describing the influence of needs on human behavior include Herzberg, who divides factors related to job satisfaction into two categories: "Satisfiers" or "Motivators," such as achievement, recognition, and increased work-related responsibility, which increase job satisfaction, and "Dissatisfiers" or "Hygiene Factors," such as poor interpersonal relations, inadequate supervision, and unsatisfactory working conditions, which increase job dissatisfaction (Herzberg, Mausner, and Synderman, 1959). Herzberg helps to place in proper perspective the various components of a volunteer's motivation by distinguishing between aspects of a position itself, which provide intrinsic satisfaction, and aspects of the context in which the job is performed, which may detract or be sources of dissatisfaction. Volunteer administrators may use this distinction to identify particular sources of satisfaction and dissatisfaction among volunteers.

McClelland (1985) identified the needs for achievement, affiliation, and power as motivators: persons responding to the need for achievement are motivated by task completion, those with a need for affiliation by interpersonal relationships, and those with a need for power by opportunities for leadership. Research findings from volunteer work generally affirm the existence of affiliation, achievement, and power needs as motivators but suggest that volunteers in different situations are likely to have those needs in different proportions. Wilson (1976) and others have encouraged volunteer administrators to use achievement, affiliation, and power to describe the motivational needs of each volunteer, the type of recognition most appropriate for each volunteer, and the focus of each volunteer position. However, Dailey (1986, p. 28) found that when compared with the organizational commitment of volunteers, "the personal characteristics of need for achievement and need for affiliation played a modest predictive role regarding job involvement. Their predictive power was insignificant relative to organizational commitment for volunteers."

McCurley and Lynch (1989) claim that the needs common to most people are belonging and autonomy, but that the needs for recognition, achievement, control, variety, growth, affiliation, power, fun, and uniqueness also influence decisions to engage in volunteer activities. Similarly, Francies (1983) reports that the following personal needs are fulfilled by volunteering: for experience, to be socially responsible, for social contact, to respond to the expectations of others, for social approval, for future rewards, and to achieve.

Although individuals' needs change over time, prompting different responses at various life stages, the availability of jobs that meet basic psychological needs provides strong inducement for volunteers.

Conscious Reasons

A second motivator is the reasons that volunteers give for involvement in volunteer organizations and programs. Some reasons provided by volunteers focus on the tasks to be performed and others focus on the location or setting in which the individual volunteers. Some reasons are focused almost entirely on client populations: altruistic responses, such as helping others and serving the community, dominate such lists. Other reasons combine altruism with self-interest, especially when the job benefits both the volunteer and others; helping to make one's community a better place in which to live and working to improve human relations, municipal services, or environmental awareness are examples. A third group of reasons focuses on the volunteers themselves: examples are deriving enjoyment from working with the client population, socializing with other volunteers, making new acquaintances, repaying benefits received, enhancing prestige, fulfilling a requirement, gaining career-related experiences, and increasing business profits.

Sherrott (1983) divides explanations for volunteering into two categories: instrumental and moral (or normative). According to the instrumental explanation, the volunteer job serves as a substitute for employment, a preparation for employment, a compensation for dissatisfying employment, an opportunity to socialize and make friends, or a constructive way to use leisure time. Moral explanations describe volunteering as a neighborly way to provide help, as an expression of religious belief, as a social duty, or as an appeasement of guilt.

In a Gallup poll, over half the volunteers gave as their reason for volunteering the desire to do something useful to help others. More than one-third said they enjoyed or had an interest in the work or activity itself. Approximately one in four knew someone who was involved in or would benefit from the activity. Over one in five had religious concerns. Nearly one in ten volunteered in order to learn and gain experience (Hodgkinson and Weitzman, 1989).

Benefits

By depicting benefits received as the incentive to volunteer, others suggest that volunteerism illustrates the main assumption of social-exchange theory, that human interactions are based on an exchange of costs for benefits. Phillips (1982), for example, interprets costs to mean what one contributes as a volunteer and benefits as what one receives. Gidron (1983) suggests that satisfaction and psychic rewards of various kinds are not simply unintentional by-products of engagement in volunteer work but are the benefits for which time and effort are exchanged.

An analysis of the expectations individuals bring to volunteer responsibilities clarifies the nature of anticipated benefits and conveys insight into volunteers' motivation. Vroom (1964) in his "expectancy theory" affirms that individuals are influenced to engage in particular activities by their perception that the performance of the activity is likely to be successful, that the performance will be recognized and rewarded, and that the outcome will have positive personal value. In other words, volunteers are likely to engage in a valued activity in which they believe they can be successful and for which they will be recognized and rewarded. By gathering information about volunteers' expectations in a systematic fashion, leaders of programs and organizations can identify the benefits anticipated by prospective volunteers and can then place those volunteers in positions that meet their expectations.

Brown and Zahrly (1989, p. 168) hypothesize that three principal kinds of reward accrue from involvement as a volunteer: "the opportunity to socialize, the opportunity to gain career-relevant skills, and the satisfaction that derives from helping to accomplish something worthwhile." Gidron (1983) classified the benefits volunteers reported as content factors (those related to the work performed) and context factors (those related to the work situation). Among the content-related benefits were the relationship with the client or patient, the performance of a significant task, the use of the volunteer's abilities and skills, and the recognition received;

context-related benefits comprised relationships with other volunteers and supervision by and assistance from professional staff.

Using volunteering as an analogue for work presents additional insight: Sherrott (1983) suggests that although paid workers receive money for their labors, volunteers receive a nonmonetary equivalent in status, recognition, and other benefits. Furthermore, Brown and Zahrly (1989, p. 173) claim that volunteers who possess strong inner direction may be able to "generate their own psychic rewards from behavior with productive outcomes" and thereby credit themselves for the results of their volunteer work.

To these general findings must be added that endless list of incentives that are program-specific, organization-specific, and person-specific and that defy neat classification but are important nevertheless. That volunteers provide public services and make other contributions to the common good with expectations of personal benefits is sufficiently well-documented to prompt leaders of volunteer programs both to identify the expectations of new and experienced volunteers and to encourage organizations to increase the benefits provided to unpaid staff members. Rewards based both on self-interest and on the interests of others seem to influence volunteer behavior positively.

Answers to the question, Why volunteer? provide useful insight into the human personality. These needs, conscious reasons, and benefits, taken together, point to both diversity and commonality in the human experience and to the needs and expectations that influence human behavior. Although the fruits of the studies cited add form and substance to an understanding of volunteer behavior, volunteer administrators must resist the temptation to reduce the complexity of motivation to a few simple ideas and thereby do great injustice to the richness and freedom of each person. At the same time, their sensitivity to the diverse needs and expectations of volunteers contributes measurably to the success of the volunteer enterprise.

Why Continue to Volunteer?

Just as volunteers have an impact on an agency or organization, on clients, and on colleagues, environments also influence volunteers.

For example, as people engage in volunteer activity, their horizons and interests may broaden, their attitudes may change, their skills may increase, and their loyalty to an organization may become stronger. Or their expectations may not be met, their skills may not be enhanced or even appropriately used, the cause may not be so compelling as first they had thought: the result is one of decreasing interest rather than fulfillment.

Thus, a person's needs and expectations may change during and as the product of a volunteer experience. Research findings must be carefully interpreted at this point. On the one hand, Brudney (1990, p. 162) points out that according to a Gallup survey "the reasons most frequently mentioned for continuing to volunteer are the same reasons most frequently mentioned for first becoming involved in a volunteer activity." On the other hand, according to McCurley and Lynch (1989) and Ilsley (1990), volunteer needs change over time and change differently for each individual. Thus, even though a person's basic reasons for volunteering may remain unchanged, one may anticipate different motivational needs at different stages of the volunteer experience.

In practice, the administrator of volunteer programs must respond to volunteer needs and expectations that change over time and with experience. Pearce (1983, p. 148) warns that "the rewards individuals expected from volunteering are often not the rewards most salient to them once they have become volunteers. Further, this shift in the rewards of volunteering, if not anticipated and managed, can result in the rapid departure of many new volunteers." Ilsley (1990, p. 31) cautions that "some organizations lose volunteers because they continually treat the volunteers as if they were new and had new volunteers' motives." Career ladders are important ways to respond to the changing needs and abilities of volunteers. Consider the following illustration:

> A volunteer administrator seeking to maintain the satisfaction of experienced volunteer facilitators of parent-education programs developed a career ladder to offer both recognition and new challenges. Once volunteers had two years of effective performance as group facilitators, they could move to positions as

trainers and, after one to two years of training experience, to positions as consultants to new trainees. For
those who did not wish to pursue the training/consul-
tation ladder, a direct-service ladder was designed; this
option involved experienced volunteers in home visits
to interview families before and after participation, as
lead facilitators after successful experience as cofacil-
itators, and in conducting and scoring tests associated
with the parent-education program. The career ladders recognized achievement and offered increased and
diverse work-related responsibility to those volunteers
who were interested and qualified.

Furthermore, organizations may be blessed with new volunteers who come with extensive experience from related paid or unpaid positions. A new volunteer may be new to volunteering, new
to a responsibility, new to an organization, or all of these. Therefore, any consideration of volunteer needs based on the presumption
of similarity in backgrounds will fail to address the diversity that
exists in any corps of volunteers.

Although it may not be feasible to assess and respond to the
needs of all volunteers on an individual basis, it is usually possible
to distinguish between new and experienced volunteers in an organization. A climate for new volunteers focuses on providing activities related to recruitment and assimilation, and planning a climate
for experienced volunteers focuses on providing activities that support their retention and offer increased responsibility.

Regardless of the volunteer's length of experience, the nature
of the volunteer responsibility (long-term, short-term, or occasional), or the relationship of the volunteer to the organization
(member, intern, youth volunteer, board member), the needs and
expectations of that person should be addressed in any plan for
motivating volunteers.

Creating a Climate That Motivates Volunteers

Climate, as we use it here, can best be described as those aspects of
an organization's culture that may influence a person's decisions

regarding volunteering. Deal and Kennedy (1982) describe corporate culture as an organization's beliefs and values, which are transmitted through employees who personify them, through rituals that symbolize them, and through an informal network by which they are reinforced and communicated. A corporate culture is also evident in how an organization operates—in the routine activities that are tied to the organization's mission. A strong corporate culture influences workers' motivation and productivity and has a positive impact on job satisfaction and retention.

The effect of an organization's culture on its ability to attract and retain volunteers is substantial because that culture communicates what the organization believes about itself, its members, its paid and unpaid staff, and its clients. These beliefs, together with the ways in which the organization's diverse parts interact to perform its mission, form a culture that may attract or repel volunteers. Dailey (1986) confirms the importance of the organization's culture in attracting volunteers through his finding that commitment to an organization often precedes job satisfaction.

The following case illustrates how an organization's culture develops volunteer commitment.

> A young woman who had been active in scouting during her youth wanted to give back something to that movement. Scouting had significantly influenced her personal development, and she was motivated to help other girls benefit from its traditions and values. She began her volunteer activities expecting to be received into a climate similar to the one that had fostered her growth and encouraged her to share with others. Her expectations were realized in the volunteer experience. Her commitment to the organization preceded her motivation to volunteer and greatly increased the likelihood that she would be satisfied with her involvement.

Although organizational leaders and administrators of volunteer programs are unable to exercise direct control over the motives of individuals, they are able to influence the overall climate of an organization or agency to promote commitment and to enhance the motivation of volunteers to accept particular positions.

Key components of an organization's climate that influence volunteer motivation are relationships within the organization, the nature and design of the responsibility or position and the opportunities available to volunteers for personal growth and development. In each of these areas, administrators and staff responsible for a volunteer program are challenged to develop ways to fulfill volunteers' needs and expectations and to allow volunteers to meet needs and to benefit from the service they provide. Development and implementation of a comprehensive plan to address the motivational needs of all volunteers are integral components of the volunteer administrator's role.

Relationships

Virtually every volunteer position contains links between the volunteer and paid staff, other volunteers, and clients. The nature of these links depends on the climate of the organization as well as on the specifics of each job. In addition, each volunteer has a relationship with the organization or agency through its leaders and administrators.

Important aspects of an organization's climate are expressed through that relationship. Descriptors such as friendly or distant, supportive or disinterested, collaborative or independent signal differences between organizations where one receives a strong sense of belonging and organizations where one can leave without being missed. When the organizational climate is good, paid staff are perceived as colleagues rather than adversaries; administrators are viewed as enabling rather than hindering; and volunteers believe that they are part of an important effort much greater than themselves.

In the following illustration, an organization recognizes the efforts of volunteers and the outcomes of their performance.

A public museum honors its volunteers with a banquet and awards ceremony each year. Paid staff members prepare and serve the meal, a speaker from the administrative staff or board of directors extols the virtues of volunteerism and the work of the volunteers, and volunteers are given awards on the basis of the total numbers of hours they have worked in the museum. Although the number of new volunteers has decreased in recent years, those veterans who gather each year at the awards banquet have a strong sense of cohesion with and recognition by the museum's paid staff and administrators. New volunteers gain a sense of the ongoing commitment of volunteers to the organization and have an opportunity to be part of a program with a strong past, present, and future.

Such events assist in the development of a climate that positively influences volunteer motivation and develops strong connections among volunteers within the organization, between volunteers and paid staff, and between the work of volunteers and the organization's mission.

Communication of the connection between the work of volunteers and the beliefs of the organization about itself and its mission is critical for fostering volunteer involvement. The relationship between volunteers and the organization is clearly evident in the attitude of organizational personnel toward volunteers and in the respect with which the organization treats volunteers. For example, volunteers who are not informed about a change in plans may correctly surmise that they are not important in the general scheme of things. However, volunteers who sense an organization's loyalty to them are likely to be motivated to return that loyalty.

Many program activities can be designed to meet the needs of new volunteers for a strong organizational relationship. Organizations can build on their public image and their success in achieving their mission. They can orient volunteers in such a way that the volunteers are both knowledgeable about the organizations and proud to be part of them. Organizations can develop commitment further by providing volunteers with information about their mission and about the opportunities for volunteer service. Pearce (1982) suggests that volunteers must perceive opportunities for personal influence in an organization prior to making a commitment to that organization.

Organizations can also recognize new volunteers in their news-letters and provide opportunities for them to be welcomed by the administration, by other volunteers, and by paid staff members. In this way they can affirm their volunteers' importance. In addition, they can provide new volunteers with signs of identification (pins, bumper stickers, sweat shirts, coffee mugs) so that they will be pub-licists for the organizations and their volunteer programs.

Furthermore, organizations can identify barriers that inhibit volunteering by particular groups of individuals. They can address obstacles, such as the need for transportation, flexible scheduling, day care, expense reimbursement, and access for the disabled, in order to provide the particular support individuals need.

Administrators of volunteer programs or volunteer leaders can visit with new volunteers to provide informal recognition, praise, and support in solving problems that may arise. They can also develop procedures to resolve conflicts and disagreements among staff members. Poor communication, misunderstandings about jobs, concern about protecting areas of responsibility, and interpersonal problems require expeditious resolution in order to limit their potentially disruptive and negative influence on an or-ganization's program and its volunteer effort. Clear procedures for the resolution of such difficulties should be in place and should be communicated to each volunteer and paid staff member.

In addition, organizations can provide informal places, such as a lounge, for volunteers, or informal occasions, such as brief social gatherings, where new volunteers can interact and build social rela-tionships with experienced volunteers. Finally, organizations can incorporate new volunteers into their written communication net-works and develop additional communication strategies for volun-teers who participate occasionally or who work on individual or off-site assignments.

Other activities can be designed to meet the needs of expe-rienced volunteers for strong organizational relationships. Organi-zations can develop contracts in which volunteers affirm their commitment over a particular time period. The contract ought to include information about responsibilities, level of achievement ex-pected, accountability, benefits of being a volunteer, and length of commitment.

Organizations can also recognize experienced volunteers for the time they have given and especially for particular contributions they have made to the achievement of the organization's mission. This recognition may be made informally in a conversation with or a note from the head of the organization, formally at a dinner or award ceremony, by nominating the person for a community volunteer-of-the-year award, or by featuring both the person and the accomplishment in the organization's newsletter. Formal recognition ceremonies reinforce the culture and climate of the organization as well as fulfill the needs and expectations of the volunteers. Informal, day-to-day means for recognizing volunteers are also important. McCurley and Lynch (1989) suggest saying thank you, showing interest in a volunteer's family and activities, sending a note of appreciation, remembering the volunteer's birthday, or celebrating the volunteer's anniversary date with the agency. Organizations can also feature the activities of volunteers in their newsletters, in national newsletters, and in local newspapers.

Organizations can structure their recognition activities by following McCurley and Lynch's (1989) "rules for recognition": Give it or volunteers will look elsewhere. Give it frequently. Give it publicly or in a peer group. Time it properly so that it comes immediately after the behavior being praised. Target the method of recognition to the needs of the person receiving it. Be consistent and sincere. Recognize achievement but praise the person.

It is also important to develop support systems for those working with difficult client populations, in stressful or dangerous situations, where the response is low, or where the task is repetitive or boring. Organizations can link volunteers in such positions with others who can be sources of encouragement.

Finally, the organization can develop communication networks that include members of the administration, the volunteer administrator, and experienced volunteers.

Volunteer Positions

A second component of organizational climate important to volunteers is the jobs they are assigned. Dailey (1986) found that task design was an important predictor of job satisfaction, which in turn was the most important determinant of commitment to the organization. This research suggests that the type and variety of volunteer tasks may be as important as the qualities of the volunteers who perform them in enhancing motivation. Organizations may be hampered in accomplishing their mission when they have limited opportunities for volunteer involvement.

In the following illustration, concern about retention forces examination of the nature and variety of volunteer options.

> A community-based organization that provides literacy training for adults was founded by a small group of dedicated tutors from area churches over twenty-five years ago. The organization has grown dramatically and now employs a professional staff, but the service to students is still provided by volunteer tutors and is the primary task assigned to volunteers. Although many of the tutors have served for several years, new tutors often leave after a few months, causing the organization to reexamine the limited options it provides for volunteer participation and to develop new positions for volunteers within the organization.

Providing several opportunities for involvement increases the potential for successful recruitment and retention of volunteers.

An organization says much about itself by what it asks volunteers to do and how it creates the positions in which they function. The degree to which volunteer jobs are clearly described in position guides, the number of different positions that exist, the expected level of performance, the connection between the position and the organization's mission, and the opportunities for moving into other volunteer positions within an agency, all convey a climate in which the contributions and the performance of volunteers are held in high regard. Being entrusted with an important responsibility and being treated with respect provide volunteers with the awareness that their expectations are matched by those of an organization or agency.

Program activities can address the needs of new volunteers for rewarding job responsibilities. For example, the organization can identify each volunteer's skills, interests, and expectations, and adapt a position so that it utilizes those specific skills and talents. Saxon and Sawyer (1984, p. 39) warn against "underplacement"— that is, requiring capable people to perform trivial tasks.

The organization can also incorporate specific goals and performance objectives in position guides so that expectations for performance and results are clearly stated. Burke and Lindsay (1985, pp. 97–98) claim that "setting difficult or challenging goals is more likely to improve performance than setting easy goals. . . . A difficult goal is more likely to encourage the worker to examine carefully the efficiency of his actions in striving for it and to be innovative and creative in finding ways to improve his efficiency."

If volunteer positions also provide autonomy and a sense of responsibility for results, volunteers are likely to attribute successful performance to their own efforts and ability.

In addition, the organization can provide job options so that new volunteers may select their area of responsibility. These options should include positions involving different tasks, levels of responsibility, lengths of commitment, and levels of skill. It is important for the organization to link each task to its goals and mission so that volunteers are able to view their responsibilities within an overall scheme. In this regard, the organization can indicate how the performance of particular tasks contributes both to its mission and to the well-being of others. Brudney (1990, p. 163) suggests placing new volunteers in positions that contribute directly to the organization's goals.

Organizations can avoid burnout by helping volunteers to set realistic performance standards, set realistic expectations for rewards, set realistic goals for achievement, and develop appropriate strategies to reach their personal goals and the goals of the organization (Bramhall, 1985). In addition, an organization can make an individual's first experience as a volunteer as positive as possible by ensuring that the job meets or exceeds the volunteer's expectations, including expectations for intrinsic rewards. This may be accomplished by developing each responsibility so that its performance is as pleasurable as possible. The organization can gather information about ways in which the volunteer's expectations are being met by providing performance-related feedback that focuses on the volunteer's job behaviors.

Program activities can also address the needs of experienced volunteers for meaningful jobs. For example, an organization can recognize that the abilities, skills, and needs of volunteers change and that careful matching of volunteers with organization needs is a continuing process. The organization can involve volunteers in the development of positions that combine various responsibilities in interesting and challenging ways.

The organization can also increase the level of autonomy, responsibility, and control in a volunteer's job in conjunction with increases in the volunteer's commitment, skill, and experience. Career ladders can provide optional areas of responsibility for experienced volunteers by building on the skill and commitment the volunteers have developed. They allow an experienced volunteer to acquire new responsibilities but to stay within the organization, and they build on a volunteer's positive and successful experiences in the organization.

In addition, the organization can provide opportunities for experienced volunteers to engage in the generation of creative ideas to solve problems, increase efficiency, and enlarge the ability of the organization to achieve its mission. The organization can also provide continuing feedback that focuses on performance-related behaviors and can adjust the level of direct supervision as a volunteer increases in skill, experience, and commitment to the organization.

In order to maintain a flexible response to volunteer needs, more than one approach can be considered in the organization of time given by volunteers. For example, Brudney (1990) suggests asking persons to set aside a number of hours weekly or monthly to perform a volunteer task. Scheier (1980a) encourages administrators of volunteer programs to consider a range of options in designing tasks, such as whether jobs should be assigned to individuals or groups of volunteers, or whether those assigned should perform them on a regular or periodic basis.

Personal Growth and Development

A third component of an organization's climate is reflected in the various opportunities it provides for volunteers to grow. Satisfaction and rewards derived from a volunteer position and the opportunity for personal growth are the pay volunteers earn. The difference between growth as a volunteer and growth as a person may not be an important distinction. Both have important positive consequences for the persons involved and may benefit the organization in which they volunteer. The provision of opportunities for growth assures volunteers that the organization values them as persons rather than as inexpensive providers of service.

In the following illustration, an opportunity for growth communicates the organization's high regard for the volunteer and at the same time enhances his value to the organization.

> A local environmental group encouraged one of its volunteer leaders to take an elective course in the management of volunteer programs as part of his university master's degree program. Furthermore, they contributed a small amount toward his tuition and books, and he used what he learned in his leadership position.

Organizations can encourage personal growth in various ways. One important activity in this regard is providing learning activities, both in formal training events and in the regular interaction between volunteers and paid professionals. Other activities that enhance volunteers' personal growth are leading training programs, representing the organization or agency in the community, assuming some responsibility for the recruitment or selection of volunteers, and providing mentoring or coaching to new volunteers. All these occasions permit volunteers to increase their knowledge and skill. In addition, good personnel management practices that involve supervision, performance appraisals, and supportive feedback also assist volunteers to increase their skill and competence.

Many program activities can fulfill the needs of new volunteers for growth and personal development. For example, the organization can provide support, supervision, and feedback to the volunteer. The volunteer administrator can discuss fears, uncertainty, and other reservations at an initial interview and through follow-up contacts in the early stages. The organization can also provide training to make certain that new volunteers are sufficiently skilled to perform the activities and can provide occasions for volunteers to attend or lead training and educational programs. The organization can design these training programs to enhance inter-personal relationships; assure development of appropriate skill levels; teach volunteers to be team members, to delegate and share responsibility, and to be supportive of the efforts of others in the organization (Bramhall, 1985). In addition, the organization can present opportunities for new volunteers to work with and learn from paid staff on a regular basis; it can assign paid staff or experienced volunteers to serve as mentors to new volunteers.

An orientation session can address volunteer needs at various levels by informing volunteers about the organization and its mission, dealing with their fears and concerns, capitalizing on their positive attitudes and enthusiasm, and providing them with a coaching or mentoring program if necessary.

Finally, the organization can encourage volunteers to develop high expectations for themselves, move toward increased levels of responsibility and effectiveness, and hold themselves responsible for their performance and their accomplishments.

Program activities can also meet the needs of experienced volunteers for growth and development. For example, the organization can reassess through interviews the needs and expectations of volunteers in order to plan for future responsibilities within the organization; it can also review each volunteer's personnel file periodically to plan for future experiences.

In addition, the organization can provide and support opportunities for volunteers to engage in continuing education; involve experienced volunteers in training, coaching, and mentoring others; provide opportunities for volunteers to broaden or increase their responsibility within the organization; and provide opportunities for volunteers to participate in planning and decision making.

Conclusion

Understanding motivation provides an administrator of volunteer programs with the tools necessary to anticipate the needs and expectations of volunteers and to respond with programs and activities designed to enhance their recruitment and retention. Enlisting new volunteers, providing them with the necessary skills, enhancing their usefulness, providing for their personal growth, and maintaining their loyalty to the organization over a period of time are key characteristics of a program that effectively motivates volunteers.

Theory and research about motivation of volunteers indicate that the decision to volunteer may be prompted by individual needs, conscious reasons, or expected benefits to oneself or to others. The needs and reasons for volunteering seem to remain constant, but expectations change as the volunteer gains experience.

Although leaders of volunteer programs are unable to exercise direct control over the motives of others, they are able to influence the climate of an organization to increase motivation. Key components here are relationships within the organization, the nature and design of the volunteer positions, and the opportunities available to a volunteer for personal growth and development.

Part Two

Working
Effectively
with
Volunteers

5

Recruiting Volunteers:
A Marketing Approach

The number of causes and organizations that rely on volunteer
staff has grown dramatically, and this trend shows no sign of
abating. The proliferation of nonprofits is in some ways beneficial
to potential volunteers because of the specialization, variety, and
healthy competition that result from large numbers. The disadvantages of this growth, however, include duplication, fragmen-
tation of resources, and an overwhelming array of choices for
financial contributors as well as for individuals and groups seeking
to volunteer their time and talents.

Competition and specialization among nonprofit organizations require that volunteer administrators further their knowledge
of those mechanisms that are effective in attracting volunteers
(Watts and Edwards, 1983). They need to satisfy the interests and
needs of prospective volunteers, who, like discriminating consumers, can choose from a multitude of alternatives in the volunteer
marketplace. Simply having a worthwhile cause and meaningful
volunteer activities to offer are no longer sufficient.

Although some speak of today's volunteer pool as shrinking,
the pool has actually been growing (Smith, 1989). Individuals are
showing renewed responsiveness to community needs and a willingness to share both their personal time and their financial resources.
A 1990 Gallup survey indicated that "Americans are showing a new
spirit of caring, evidenced by sharp increases in giving and volunteering among most segments of society, a growing positive attitude

toward community service, and a swelling majority of the baby boom generation giving time and money to charitable causes" (Independent Sector, 1990). Today's volunteer pool includes women who are employed in professions outside the home; youth; corporate volunteers; individuals who have retired at an earlier age and who have longer, healthier lives than their parents; and persons from diverse racial and cultural groups.

To remain competitive in this changing volunteer market, administrators must be able to employ recruitment strategies that have maximum potential for successfully attracting volunteers whose skills and interests match the needs of the organization. The volunteer administrator who approaches volunteer recruitment as a marketing problem and uses exchange theory and other principles of marketing to gain the attention of potential volunteers will remain competitive in the most demanding environment.

Volunteers as Consumers: A Marketing Approach

It may seem inappropriate and out of keeping with the spirit of volunteerism to refer to volunteers as consumers. Are volunteers not, after all, givers rather than users of services? Benefactors rather than recipients? Although varying degrees of altruism distinguish volunteer efforts, the principles of marketing and exchange theory normally associated with the corporate sector are also relevant to the voluntary sector.

Decisions related to volunteer involvement are akin to those involved in a consumer's purchase of a product. One first learns of a product through some form of advertising or from another person. One then assesses the qualities of the product to determine whether the purchase will satisfy a need or enrich one's life to a degree that justifies its cost. As prospective volunteers select both the organization with which they will be involved and the type of position in which they will function, they make comparisons, weigh alternatives, and assess advantages and disadvantages in much the same way that a consumer approaches a purchase. Just as consumers search for and select products, prospective volunteers search for and select meaningful ways to give of their time and talents.

Consumers seek to maintain a healthy ratio of benefits to

costs, and volunteers typically seek (consciously or unconsciously) to keep the benefits of volunteering above the perceived costs. Those positions whose return is greater than the investment required are more readily filled than those with a lesser return. In volunteerism, an equitable exchange is one in which an experience of value is gained for a contribution of value. Vineyard (1984) suggests that organizations offering a combination of experiences that provide both tangible and intangible rewards to prospective volunteers will have greater success in attracting them.

The rewards and benefits of volunteering are often difficult to describe and quantify. Knowing that one's efforts made the difference in the life of a youngster or having the sense of personal growth that results from facilitating a peer support group are examples of volunteer rewards and benefits that, as commodities, are difficult and perhaps impossible to quantify. In the following illustration a volunteer administrator emphasizes the rewards of the volunteer experience.

> A volunteer administrator for a child-abuse prevention program promoted the rewards of involvement in her program to prospective volunteers as follows: You will help reduce the potential for child abuse in at-risk families; your one-on-one work with parents will increase their belief in alternatives to physical punishment; you will receive twenty-four hours of classroom instruction and forty-eight hours of on-the-job training from social workers with master's degrees. On successful completion of the training program, you will be able to add to your resume the credential "Certified Community Educator." A letter of reference from this agency will be available to you on request.

Many organizations and causes approach volunteer recruitment primarily from the standpoint of the needs of the organization and fail to understand the need to maintain the delicate balance between organizational and volunteer needs. In the following illustration, a library seeks individuals who will work at the convenience of the organization and its paid staff.

A public library began a program in which the role of the volunteer was to read books aloud, making audio-tapes for use by the blind. However, after six months of operation, the program had only a handful of active volunteers. The librarian decided to bring together a small group of experienced volunteer administrators and staff from the local volunteer center to help her examine what she referred to as "a recruitment prob-lem." After a brief discussion, the group concluded that the problem lay not in recruitment but in the fact that the library staff involved in the program were available for interviewing, training, and supervising volunteers only during daytime hours on weekdays. When that situation changed, volunteer involvement in this satisfying, meaningful program increased dramatically.

Organizations that approach prospective volunteers as con-sumers and use principles of marketing to attract and retain them will achieve volunteer involvement that is mutually beneficial. Contrary to commonly held misconceptions, marketing is not simply promo-tions, advertising gimmicks, or public relations. Rather, marketing encompasses conducting market research; analyzing potential markets; setting goals and objectives; and devising, selecting, and using persuasive communication techniques to promote the product effectively. According to A. R. Kratchenberg (cited in Stone and Hansen-Stone, 1987), "Marketing deals with . . . uncovering specific needs, satisfying those needs by development of appropriate goods and services, letting people know of their availability, and offering them at the appropriate prices, at the right time and place." Volunteer administrators who view potential volunteers as prospective consu-mers and design programs to meet their needs have taken the first step toward a recruitment program that is market-driven.

Market Research

Market-driven volunteer-recruitment efforts are built on an in-depth understanding of the volunteer marketplace. Every organization needs more and better information than it has about its current and potential volunteers, and market research provides that information by linking the organization with its market environment (Aaker and Day, 1983). Information is needed about potential volunteers' perceptions and needs; competitor strategies; and the technological, social, political, and cultural developments and demographic trends that affect current and potential recruits. Through analysis and interpretation of information gathered from the marketplace, organizations can identify opportunities and develop courses of action that will position the organization to attract prospective volunteers.

Information on the volunteer marketplace can be gained in a variety of ways, the simplest being examination of information obtained from national and local studies conducted by foundations, planning groups, researchers, and volunteer centers. Such organizations often publish reports that provide data on who volunteers, where they volunteer, their motivation for involvement, and how they were recruited.

> A volunteer administrator learned from a local study that companies that participate in annual community employee-giving campaigns also support and encourage employee volunteerism. She obtained a list of those companies and their volunteer coordinators, and contacted them to learn how she could present employees with information about volunteer opportunities within her organization. Some companies allowed her to include a brochure in employee pay envelopes, and others provided space in their monthly employee newsletter to advertise for specific volunteer positions. One company invited her to a meeting of their employee involvement team to discuss possible group projects.

Market research can also involve gathering information from current and potential volunteers.

> A volunteer center with a ten-year history of managing an active corporate volunteer program was seeing

little growth in the number and variety of companies in the program. Its board of directors developed a task force to study the program and discover the barriers to growth. A volunteer from a market research firm was recruited to conduct a series of focus groups consisting of decision makers from active corporate volunteer programs as well as managers from companies having no formal volunteer program. Feedback gained through this market research project resulted in the development of new approaches to the recruitment of companies as well as the development of new types of volunteer opportunities for the corporate sector.

Vineyard (1984) suggests that market research include identification of the publics with whom the organization would like to establish an exchange relationship. This step involves developing a list of individuals and groups that make up those publics and identifying members who will be helpful in recruitment efforts among these groups. Vineyard recommends compiling a "resource inventory" that connects the volunteer administrator and others in the organization to potential volunteer publics via individuals who are connected with the organization in some way. These individuals may be direct-service volunteers, committee members, board members, staff, families of staff, and funders. They can serve as spokespersons for the organization or can help the volunteer administrator gain access to groups of potential volunteers.

Use of such a resource inventory requires that volunteer administrators and others involved in the recruitment effort become aware of the interests and motivations of those they wish to recruit before approaching them. Current volunteer opportunities must be examined to assess how to match them to the known interests of prospective volunteers and how to communicate their value.

Market Segmentation

Weinstein (1987) believes that segmentation is the key to marketing success. The objective of segmentation research is to analyze markets, find a niche for one's product or service, and develop and capitalize on this superior, competitive position. Market segmentation involves partitioning markets into discrete segments of potential consumers who have similar characteristics and who are likely to exhibit similar volunteer interests. Use of market segmentation requires delineating the various market populations, such as youth, the elderly, service groups, employee groups, men, the unemployed, college students, and then employing separate volunteer-recruitment strategies that target each. A profile for each market population is developed so that volunteer positions can be readily matched to the interests, needs, motivation, and availability of each segment. The profile includes information on the volunteer position, characteristics of those most likely to be interested, and suggestions for how to attract those individuals.

Such targeted marketing is based on the premise that everyone is not a prospect for every product or service. It is impossible for any organization to pursue every market opportunity; thus strategic choices must be made. Because organizations need to use their resources efficiently, they must target their recruitment efforts to the most likely prospects.

Heidrich (1990) examined market segmentation as applied to the problem of volunteer recruitment and retention and concluded that knowledge of volunteers' life-styles leads to the effective targeting of particular groups. Heidrich's study concentrated on four types of volunteer: provider of *direct service*—club leader, coach, home visitor, counselor; *leader*—officer, board member, committee chair, project leader, fundraiser; provider of *general support*—office worker, cleaner, receptionist; and *member at large*—someone who occasionally attends meetings or activities. She found that these particular roles within organizations attract volunteers with similar life-styles: each group is distinguished by how its members spend their time, by what is important to them, by their opinions about the world, and by their socioeconomic and demographic status. For example, volunteers attracted to leadership roles were likely to have attended college, to be self-directed, and to be interested in complex issues and problems.

Targeted recruitment is based on assumptions about what motivates members of selected groups. However, Lynch (1990) and Weinstein (1987) suggest that volunteer administrators use caution when generalizing about various groups. Segmentation findings provide a composite profile of a group but do not describe an individual's behavior or decision to volunteer. Prospective volunteers may share a common socioeconomic and demographic profile but may have different interests, attitudes, and perspectives on life.

Marketing Mix

A consumer-oriented approach to marketing recognizes that volunteer recruitment is best approached through a variety of strategies. Stone and Hansen-Stone (1987) suggest using a combination of undifferentiated marketing, differentiated marketing, and concentrated marketing.

Undifferentiated marketing assumes that everyone is alike in their needs and motivations for volunteering. No attempt is made to distinguish subgroups or tailor recruitment messages to specific audiences. This approach usually uses altruism as the common element by promoting volunteer involvement as the way to give of oneself to others. Broad, rather generic recruitment messages, such as "Be Involved," "Make a Difference," "Find Joy in Giving," or "Your Help is Needed" are characteristic of those used in an undifferentiated marketing approach.

Differentiated marketing recognizes the existence of market segments and develops a variety of volunteer positions and recruitment messages based on their unique needs and interests. A church that understands the concept of differentiated marketing will make special recruitment appeals for volunteer positions designed for teens, singles, older adults, parents, males, and females, and other groups within the congregation. Singles may be recruited for positions that are group-oriented and that clearly offer an opportunity to meet new people. Teens may be recruited for positions that are recreational in nature, such as supervising children's games at a church fair. A different appeal is made specifically to each group for whom the volunteer position is designed.

Concentrated marketing recognizes the value of a differentiated marketing approach but acknowledges that most organizations have limited resources. A concentrated marketing approach targets one market segment at a time to reach prospective volunteers possessing that particular profile. For example, a museum volunteer administrator who was seeking individuals to give guided tours to school groups concentrated her marketing efforts on retired schoolteachers. She arranged for newspaper articles that featured several retired teachers who were currently involved, encouraged current volunteers to recruit their retired co-workers, spoke at a meeting of the local retired teachers' association, and arranged for recruitment flyers to be available at each meeting of the group.

The most appropriate marketing strategy to employ necessarily depends on the needs of the organization and its volunteer positions, as illustrated by the following case:

> A volunteer administrator needed to recruit volunteers to help homebound clients with basic assistance in managing personal finances. She realized that an undifferentiated approach appealing to volunteers in the community at large probably would not locate individuals with the particular knowledge and skills required. Therefore, she chose a concentrated approach by targeting individuals employed in accounting and banking. Flexible time schedules made it possible for full-time employees to be involved. Volunteer interviews and orientation were available evenings and Saturdays.

Many organizations have a natural constituency from which to recruit. Educational and youth-serving organizations may have an obvious source of volunteers in the form of parents. Organizations having a clear source of volunteers can focus on concentrated marketing strategies, while those relying on a broad base of potential volunteers must design a mix of recruitment efforts. The challenge to the volunteer administrator is to identify market segments and use appropriate marketing strategies.

Recruitment Mechanisms

Lynch (1990) recommends using a volunteer who is a member of the targeted group as a spokesperson in recruitment efforts. This person can help prepare a message that focuses on common interests and needs. The following sample of a recruitment effort informs a particular population of potential volunteers how their needs will be met.

> A volunteer administrator at an animal welfare orga-
> nization approached a current teen volunteer about
> how other teens might best be recruited The teen sug-
> gested that the two of them make a presentation to the
> community-service class at her high school and volun-
> teered to write an article about her most rewarding
> and fun experiences at the humane society for her
> school newspaper.

Ensman (1984) suggests recruiting volunteers through an annual appeal, modeled on the traditional annual fund drive. An annual appeal focuses energy and can save both time and money. It allows for significant media involvement and is best used when a large number of volunteer opportunities are available. From the standpoint of prospective volunteers, the annual appeal is ideal. The organization can develop a catalog of positions for volunteers including position guides. The annual appeal can be conducted via mail through use of a recruitment letter or brochure about volunteer opportunities, a response device, and a reply envelope. Ensman suggests developing a tradition of conducting such a drive at a given time each year, perhaps during National Volunteer Week.

Personal contact, such as a direct request from a friend or family member, is the primary way people become involved in voluntary activities. A study of human service organizations conducted by Watts and Edwards (1983) showed that 94 percent used word of mouth as a primary means of volunteer recruitment. People are likely to give and to volunteer when directly asked, and the inability to refuse when asked accounts for a significant part of volunteers' reasons for undertaking their assignment. According to Independent Sector (1990), 87 percent of those asked to volunteer say yes.

Personal contact as a means of recruitment has a serious drawback: it may limit participation to a closed segment of the population. People ask those whom they know, and they usually know people most like themselves. In addition to not complying with affirmative-action guidelines, this form of recruitment fails to attract a diverse group of volunteers to an organization.

In their study of volunteer recruitment, Watts and Edwards (1983) found that only 56 percent of the organizations surveyed used mass media to recruit volunteers, even though the vast majority of them found it to be effective. Its effectiveness depends on its ability to target particular audiences and to present enough information to help them determine whether the volunteer position matches their interests and skills. Mass media appears to be an underutilized recruitment source because of perceptions of volunteer administrators about its cost and effectiveness. Volunteer administrators perceive word-of-mouth recruitment to be an inexpensive and more effective method.

Size and resources are the two primary factors that determine the type of recruitment mechanisms used by organizations. Small agencies frequently do not have sufficient resources to use mass media and may be hampered in other forms of recruiting by limited numbers of paid staff. They also may not be able to afford the types of incentives larger organizations are able to offer to volunteers, such as reimbursement for transportation and child care, meals, and stipends. Volunteer administrators in larger organizations often have the advantage of access to communications and public-relations staff with whom to consult and who can help with volunteer-recruitment efforts. Membership organizations may be limited to their constituency as the chief source of volunteers.

Recruitment in a Pluralistic Society

According to the VOLUNTEER 2000 study conducted by the American Red Cross (Smith, 1989), the pool of volunteers in the United States has been growing. A larger percentage of women employed outside the home, who were expected to drop out of the volunteer force, are now involved in volunteer activities than woman working as full-time homemakers. Students in schools and colleges have shown renewed interest in volunteering. Organizations of retirees are, more than ever, promoting volunteerism through talent banks and networks. Increased interest in religion has resulted in the growth of volunteer activities sponsored by religious groups. Corporations are strongly encouraging community service by their employees, and government at all levels has stimulated interest in and recognition of volunteer work.

What has not developed to a substantial degree is increased participation by those groups that may face barriers to involvement in formal volunteer activities: ethnic and racial minorities; low-income, disabled, and homebound individuals; and individuals lacking access to transportation. Large pools of such unutilized or underutilized people exist in most communities. As diverse populations enter communities, their integration is important not only as consumers of service but also as service providers. According to Schindler-Rainman (1986), it cannot be emphasized too often that today's administrators absolutely must know how to tap into the pluralistic resources of the community. She encourages volunteer administrators to go beyond the incumbent groups and consciously seek persons with different racial and cultural backgrounds, values, skills, and time availabilities.

As early as the year 2000, people of cross-cultural backgrounds will make up the majority of the population in fifty-three of North America's one hundred largest cities and will comprise 29 percent of the workforce (Smith, 1989). By the turn of the century, one of every three North Americans will be of Latino, African American, Asian/Pacific Islander, or Middle Eastern descent. This demographic shift from a predominantly white to a diverse racial and ethnic population will affect volunteerism. Ellis and Noyes (1990) present a host of material on the history of volunteer involvement by minority populations; they have most frequently focused their activities on issues facing particular racial and ethnic groups— housing, employment, and other civil rights issues. Minorities also have a long tradition of involvement in volunteer groups that are parallel to, yet separate from, those of the majority population, such as trade and professional associations, women's and men's clubs, and unions. Despite this long tradition of volunteerism, minorities are underrepresented in the volunteer programs of many of today's organizations.

Volunteer administrators who make a special effort to attract minority volunteers will reap a number of benefits. Recruitment and development of a diverse volunteer workforce can help cut program costs and increase the productivity of seriously underused human resources (Nestor, 1991). In addition, a diverse group can be given an opportunity to receive the benefits of participating in volunteer work. When minorities volunteer, the organization benefits from an expanded range of perspectives and opinions.

A number of barriers limit the involvement of minority groups. First, recruitment information, both verbal and written, is typically in English only. Some languages lack a word similar in meaning to *volunteer,* while in some cultures a negative association is attached to volunteers. Second, certain aspects of the volunteer world are foreign to some cultures. Organization and committee structures, working outside of one's religious community or local neighborhood, and what may seem like intrusion into the private lives of others may require interpretation to certain groups. Third, low-income persons are willing to work in causes they believe in, but they cannot afford to incur related expenses, such as the cost of transportation, telephones, child or elder care, training, and uniforms. Fourth, not all volunteer opportunities are located at handicap-accessible sites; lack of ways to communicate with hearing- or sight-impaired persons may also be a barrier to involvement. Fifth, too many volunteer opportunities are available only on weekdays during normal working hours. Sixth, too few opportunities exist for couples and families.

Chambre (1982, p. 4) claims that "minority volunteers can be recruited using the same techniques as those used for all volunteers. However, some special efforts must also be made and volunteer administrators must be sensitive to the unique needs of minority volunteers." For example, a significant gap in time between initial contact and assuming the volunteer role may unintentionally signal to potential minority volunteers that they are not wanted. A shortened screening and orientation process may be important because minority volunteers are generally sensitive to negative cues during these stages. Minority volunteers are especially sensitive to any implication that screening is intended to exclude individuals. If extensive screening is necessary, its rationale and relevance should be made clear.

Chambre also recommends that when recruiting African

American and Hispanic volunteers, organizations should show how their goals and methods are consistent with the needs and interests of people in these minority communities. Volunteer roles must be presented as ways to achieve these mutual goals. She suggests communicating the general need for volunteers while at the same time mentioning the special value of minority participation. In addition, when organizations indicate the number of minority volunteers being sought, potential volunteers are likely to respond out of the belief that their contribution will be significant.

Lynch (1983) recommends that recruitment for diversity involve identification of the minority population to be recruited, analysis of their motives for volunteer involvement, and development of volunteer positions designed especially to meet their needs and promote their interests. Promotional efforts should also indicate to the potential volunteers that the organization is both an appropriate and a comfortable place. Low participation by minorities in the volunteer activities of organizations may result from their perception that the organizations are difficult to enter rather than from a lack of motivation to volunteer. According to Nestor and Fillichio (1991), minority volunteers may be "pioneering" by moving into an organization outside their neighborhood, and they may need a special welcome in order to feel comfortable. At the same time, the success of these volunteers affects the ability of the organization to attract additional people from culturally diverse backgrounds.

Cultural sensitivity on the part of the volunteer administrator is also a key factor in the successful recruitment of minority volunteers. Nestor (1984) offers suggestions that are helpful when developing recruitment strategies directed toward Hispanics: Use the Church, one of the predominant societal influences for Hispanics. Include entire families in intergenerational groups to make volunteer involvement a family activity. And translate brochures and other printed material into Spanish, using photos of Hispanic families.

In addition, volunteer administrators may need to make other adjustments in order to integrate Spanish-speaking volunteers into their programs, such as designing volunteer positions especially for Spanish-speaking individuals, conducting training in

Spanish, and translating printed materials (including the volunteer application form and other forms to be completed by volunteers) into Spanish.

In order to involve minority volunteers successfully, an organization must publicly make it a priority and recruit people of color for both paid and volunteer leadership positions. Nestor (1984) cites the need to be prepared for resistance on the part of current staff and suggests that an organization seeking Hispanic volunteers collaborate with agencies having well-established links to the Hispanic community.

Chambre (1982) recommends use of a combination of one-to-one contacts and mass media to recruit minority volunteers. She suggests newspaper feature stories that highlight the efforts of minority volunteers as a way to attract others. She also recommends establishing a collaborative relationship with local minority groups to recruit minority volunteers. Through the collaborative relationship, the volunteer administrator promotes awareness of the organization's purpose and develops trust between members of the two organizations. Then recruitment through one-to-one contacts begins.

According to Sills (1957), the decision to volunteer often involves a "trigger event," which transforms vague interests and intentions into tangible action. Most often, the trigger event involves another person known to the volunteer. The actions of this person may crystallize a decision to volunteer that has been under consideration for a period of time. Data from a study conducted in Pennsylvania by Nehnevajsa and Kareletz (1976) indicate that African Americans, significantly more than whites, often rely on other individuals to trigger their decision to volunteer. This reliance on others is probably due to the limited experience of minorities with voluntary organizations and with organizations outside their own community. Other individuals provide reassurance to the potential volunteers that they are qualified, that the role is appropriate, and that the organization will be receptive.

The volunteer administrator can, by recognizing the decision-making process involved in stepping forward to volunteer, develop recruitment strategies that assist potential volunteers in crystallizing their decisions. These recruitment strategies may include asking influential community leaders to identify and nominate potential volunteers and holding social gatherings of current and potential volunteers.

Conclusion

Volunteer recruitment is best approached as a marketing process involving research, planning, and implementation. A targeted approach designed to reach segments of the population whose interests, needs, and goals are likely to match those of an organization is likely to achieve greater success than a generic, undifferentiated approach to the community as a whole. Whatever mechanism is being used as a volunteer-recruitment tool, it must accurately portray the volunteer position and the mission of the organization.

Volunteer administrators and their organizations will attract increased numbers of volunteers if they develop volunteer opportunities and recruitment techniques that appeal to an increasingly culturally diverse population. However, current paid and volunteer staff may need assistance in enhancing their cultural sensitivity before minority volunteers become a significant part of the volunteer workforce.

6

Training and Development for Volunteers: Keys to Effectiveness

Administrators of volunteer programs constantly face the challenge of making the most of the human resources available to them, particularly as the demand for volunteer services increases more rapidly than the supply of volunteers. This challenge requires the ability both to attract volunteers and to prepare them to perform their responsibilities. The process by which organizations maximize the human resources available to them and increase the value of those volunteers, both to the volunteers themselves and to the organization, is staff development. Recruitment induces persons to become involved in an organization; placement locates volunteers in appropriate positions; but the learning process converts the raw material of human resources into the valuable asset on which every nonprofit organization depends.

Volunteers generally have varying levels of knowledge about an organization and of skills applicable to its program. The first gathering of any group of new volunteers, whether the new-member class at a church, the new home-support team at the hospice, or the new board of directors of the Little League, requires the administrator of volunteer programs (by any title) to see beyond the volunteers' inexperience and newness, just as the diamond cutter ponders the creation of something of great value out of rough raw material.

Staff development provides opportunities for learning that result in increased knowledge, the acquisition of new skills, or changes in attitudes or values on the part of staff, paid or unpaid.

According to Ilsley (1989), the type of learning program provided depends to a great degree on the organizational context and on the experience of the volunteer learner. Some learning occurs through formal activities initiated and directed by the organization's leaders and presented as training events and classes. Other learning is informal—on-the-job training, self-directed activities, or events where learning is secondary to other purposes. An important task of the person responsible for coordinating staff-development activities is to encourage participation in formal and informal learning activities and the integration of both into the volunteer experience. This chapter will examine the why, when, what, how, and who of a comprehensive volunteer-development program.

Value of Educational Programs

The value of any staff-development program must be weighed against its cost to the organization, and its cost to the volunteers, and the consequences of not providing such activities. The cost of providing such a program is usually measured by calculating paid and unpaid staff time, the dollar value of ancillary expenses, and the time volunteers spend in learning rather than in service activities. The cost of training to the volunteers themselves is measured by the time they are involved in staff development activities; by the energy required to develop new attitudes, knowledge, and skills; by the value of any activities that may be neglected in favor of the training; and by the increased commitment their development in an organization signifies. The cost of not providing a program is measured by poor performance, poor utilization of skills, high volunteer turnover, low regard for volunteers, volunteers' inadequate knowledge of the organization's purpose and function, and poor representation of the organization in the community by its volunteers.

Benefits to an organization derived from a comprehensive volunteer-development program include the following:

• Volunteers who possess accurate information about the organization; its purpose, program, and needs; and the issues confronting it.

- Volunteers who represent the organization in the community in an accurate and positive manner.
- Volunteers who are well-informed about their responsibilities in the organization and who have the knowledge and skills necessary to perform their jobs correctly and efficiently.
- Volunteers who are knowledgeable about the resources available for and necessary to the performance of their jobs.
- Volunteers whose training reduces the liability incurred by their activity in the organization.
- Volunteers who are highly motivated, loyal to the organization, socialized in its culture, and committed to its cause.
- Volunteers who are capable of working independently within the organization and who can help other volunteers.
- Volunteers who are familiar with the operation of the organization and who possess the knowledge and skills to fill many different positions within it.
- Volunteers who have a high level of ownership of the organization and its mission and can inspire other volunteers with their enthusiasm and commitment.
- Volunteers who are regular in attendance, who consistently perform well, and who have a positive attitude toward their work.

In addition to providing benefits to an organization, staff-development programs also provide benefits to volunteers that add significantly to the rewards of volunteer work. The following are examples of benefits volunteers receive from staff development:

- Job-related skills and knowledge that can be used in other positions, both paid and unpaid.
- Personal growth, especially increased confidence and competence.
- Recognition as valuable assets of an organization because of ability to take on broadened responsibilities.
- Selection for advanced positions on the organization's volunteer career ladder.
- Preparation for a variety of other life experiences.
- Recognition of value and worth as individuals.

Some organizations excel in the use of their training programs as vehicles to attract potential volunteers. One danger of staff-development programs known widely for their high quality is that persons may volunteer in order to receive the training rather than to be prepared to provide service: Filinson (1988) describes a training program in which participants were instructed about aging and were equipped to provide services to frail, homebound elderly, but only half of those trained were interested in volunteering. Programs that teach broadly applicable skills, such as water safety, cardiopulmonary resuscitation, leadership, or identification of antique and art objects may be particularly susceptible to higher than average attrition between training and direct service. Volunteer administrators have addressed this problem by developing contracts with trainees, assessing a charge for training, and using selective recruitment techniques.

Occasions for Learning Activities

Five principal needs supply occasions for providing learning activities to volunteers: the need to learn about the organization; the need to possess skills and knowledge to undertake a particular job; the need to be updated about changes in the position, the organization, or the clients; the need to prepare for increased responsibility within an organization; and the need for personal growth and enrichment. Programs that address more than one of these needs or that address personal growth needs along with organizational needs are likely to be particularly attractive to volunteers.

Learning About the Organization

Acquainting a volunteer with an organization is a learning process, not an isolated educational event. The process begins with the volunteer's initial formal and informal encounters with the organization—receiving public information about the group, having conversations with other volunteers, and being interviewed by staff members or the volunteer coordinator. As a result of these contacts, most new volunteers come with some knowledge of the organization's program and some notion of how they may be able to participate in it.

This process continues with planned learning events, often

called orientation or welcoming sessions. The chief purpose of these activities is to provide information about the organization and to initiate the new volunteer into its culture. The information may be provided through a lecture, videotape, slides, or written material. Topics typically include the organization's philosophy, history, and traditions; the importance of its mission; how it is organized and funded; how it operates; various opportunities for volunteer involvement; and how volunteers and paid staff cooperate to achieve the organization's mission. No orientation is complete without an introduction to the organization's rules and procedures or its system of accountability.

Many organizations have gathered this material into a manual for volunteers. Such a practice may avoid having volunteers overwhelmed with information at an orientation session. More important, it provides the necessary information in written form so that volunteers may read and refer to it at a later date. For liability purposes, possession of a policy manual provides tangible evidence that the volunteer received information about organizational policy and behavior.

When vital information about the organization is presented in written form, orientation may include time for socialization as well as instruction—welcoming new volunteers to the program, helping them gain a sense of the organization, having them meet new and experienced paid and unpaid staff, and giving them a tour of the facility. The socialization process assimilates new volunteers into the organization so that they feel that they belong, that they are part of a team, and that the organization's mission is their work.

Many effective orientation programs also emphasize the organization's expectations of volunteers, dwelling on conduct, accountability, and responsibility. Brudney (1990, p. 195) recommends "informing [people] fully of the expectations for volunteering . . . so that [they] can make reasoned choices about donating time." The importance of orientation in setting the stage for a successful volunteer/organization relationship has led many organizations to insist that volunteers complete this process before being assigned to and trained for a particular position.

Many volunteers work with populations such as the terminally ill, disabled children, incarcerated individuals, persons with different cultural or socioeconomic backgrounds, and abused individuals. Working with groups and individuals with severe needs requires explicit examination of the emotional demands of such work and of the attitudes and values that potential volunteers may bring. Some researchers (Filinson, 1988; Hayslip and Walling, 1985-1986) have had limited success changing the attitudes of potential volunteers toward members of the population served; others (Wilkinson and Wilkinson, 1986-1987) have been successful in altering attitudes of volunteers so that they can cope with the demands of working with needy clients. Some organizations use orientation to confront potential volunteers with the challenges such as these that are inherent in the program.

Because time constraints in an orientation program limit the amount of information that can be shared, it is usually effective for such a program to provide a background against which additional information may be assimilated in the future. Over the long term, a continuing information flow about the organization and its work reinforces a volunteer's commitment to the mission and clients of the organization.

Learning About a Particular Job

Preparing volunteers for particular tasks builds on the skills, knowledge, and motivation they bring. In response to the need for additional preparation, staff development may include formal training events and informal educational activities, such as observation, mentoring, or on-the-job training, depending on the nature of the job to be learned and how much of it volunteers already know or can do.

The precise design of a program of learning about a particular job depends on several factors: the number of volunteers to be trained, the amount of time available, and the background and experience of the volunteers. For example, greater numbers of trainees make individualized instruction more difficult; more experienced trainees require less time. Perhaps the most critical element is the nature and complexity of the task. As Marsick (1988) notes, the emphasis in some positions is on standardization of performance; in these cases all volunteers are taught to perform the tasks in identical ways. In other positions, the emphasis is on the ability of the volunteer to exercise appropriate judgment in response to a problem or situation. Learning a standardized procedure requires demonstrating the task and having the volunteer practice it until established performance standards are met. Learning to exercise judgment requires having the volunteer make decisions in simulated situations that are as close as possible to those the volunteer will encounter in the program.

Formal educational programs followed by on-the-job training link understanding of a task with the capability to perform it. Mentoring and coaching are techniques frequently used to help persons interpret their experience and to build upon their failures and successes. In this example, a clear presentation of theory, rationale, and procedures precedes the opportunity to use skills and knowledge.

> Following a two-day orientation and training program for volunteer tutors in an adult literacy program, each new tutor works with a veteran tutor in a three-phase process. During the first week, the new tutor observes the experienced tutor working with adult students. During the second week, the new tutor and the experienced tutor work together, the experienced tutor serving as a coach. During the succeeding weeks, the new tutor works alone, but the experienced tutor is available as a mentor to provide seasoned counsel, support, and assistance with problem solving.

This process incorporates both coaching, as the new tutor observes and receives feedback from the experienced tutor, and mentoring, as the expertise of the veteran is made available to the new tutor.

Often organizations assume that people learn best by experience and that volunteers with little or no formal training can master a job as they perform it. Such a practice does not guarantee that volunteers will be able to analyze their experience in order to learn from it or that their learning will contribute to their practice.

This approach has the potential for disastrous consequences: the program may be seriously damaged by inadequate performance, and the mission of the organization may be unrealized simply because volunteers fail to learn from their experience. When placed in new positions and left to their own devices, many volunteers learn that the organization places a low priority on quality performance and on preparing volunteers for it.

Elkins and Cohen (1982) demonstrated the limit to learning on the job by isolating the effects of prejob training and on-the-job experience for nonprofessional volunteer counselors in a telephone crisis-intervention program. They found that skills and knowledge increased significantly with prejob training but did not improve with five months of on-the-job experience. They concluded that experience does not automatically increase skills and knowledge in crisis counseling.

These limitations notwithstanding, volunteers judge the informal learning that occurs as a volunteer job is performed to be highly significant. According to Ilsley (1990, p. 99), "The learning that matters most . . . comes . . . from conversations with other volunteers or their own experience."

On-the-job experience may require prejob training for it to make a significant contribution to staff development. But organizations do not give volunteers the best on-the-job learning opportunities when they assign only menial tasks or provide only minimal supervisory assistance. One advantage of on-the-job training is that it allows supervisors an early opportunity to observe how a trainee performs a task. Volunteers whose abilities fail to match position responsibilities may be provided with alternative opportunities before they become discouraged or the organization becomes dissatisfied with their performance.

Staff development focused on a particular job also includes providing information about the organizational context: With whom will the volunteer work? To whom is the volunteer accountable? How is the volunteer supervised? What are the criteria for satisfactory performance? What arrangements has the organization made (such as access to parking, provision of maps, and introduction to coworkers) to accommodate a new volunteer? Volunteers also need to know what resources are available to them and how they can be obtained.

Learning About Changes and Transitions

As much as administrators work to keep their programs stable, it is virtually impossible to eliminate the changes that pervade every volunteer effort: changes in clients, settings, paid or unpaid staff, relationships, accountability, policies, and definitions of responsibility occur periodically in every program. Although such changes may be needed to increase the efficiency and effectiveness of a volunteer effort or simply to respond to changing internal and external forces that affect a program, they will not be successful without careful planning. Volunteers often view changes as disruptions, criticisms, or even intrusions into "their" program. At worst, volunteers' dissatisfaction or resistance may cause them to ignore or sabotage program changes and set them against the leaders of the organization. Furthermore, negative responses to change may diminish the quality of service and lower levels of productivity.

Volunteer-development programs can promote the successful implementation of change in several ways: by increasing among volunteers the skills and knowledge required by changes in responsibility; by identifying the sources and rationale for change; by involving volunteers in planning for change; by developing attitudes among volunteers that support change; by providing support for volunteers during periods of uncertainty and transition; by engaging volunteers in solving problems change may cause. In general, volunteers can be prepared for new responsibilities in a changed environment and incorporated into the change process so that their voices are heard and their motivation and commitment are maintained throughout.

Learning About Increased Responsibilities

A fourth purpose for which learning activities are developed is to prepare volunteers for increased responsibility in the organization. Volunteer programs with career ladders offer diverse and advanced opportunities to experienced volunteers.

As organizations assess their future leadership needs, they can identify volunteers with the experience and potential to become recruiters, trainers, and supervisors of volunteers; representatives of the organization in the community; or members of policy-making bodies. On the basis of this assessment, organizations can select potential volunteer leaders and develop a plan for them to acquire the necessary skills and knowledge.

Successful implementation of a development program that prepares volunteers for future responsibilities serves the organization by ensuring smooth transitions during changes in volunteer personnel. It serves volunteers equally well by rewarding them for faithful work and by identifying the steps to future responsibilities. Training for the future becomes an intermediate step on the career ladder for them and provides motivation to remain with an organization.

The following illustration shows how one organization developed a career ladder within a parent-education program.

> The program manager created a training program to prepare successful minority-client "graduates" to serve as volunteer peer-parent educators. The program included twenty-four hours of classroom instruction followed by fourteen weeks of on-the-job training in which trainees served as cofacilitators under the direct supervision of an experienced parent educator. After approximately one year's service, these volunteers could become "lead facilitators," a position of increased responsibility that included training of new clients-turned-volunteer staff.

This career ladder offers several benefits: clients are empowered to serve others; clients' learning is reinforced through their volunteer experience; services are delivered by a competent, culturally diverse staff; and volunteers have an opportunity to establish themselves in a career that they can be paid for in the future.

The development of volunteer leaders is unfortunately often unattended to until an urgent need arises. If the planning is done in a timely fashion, however, many benefits accrue. The creation of a plan for leadership development provides the opportunity and structure for careful selection of personnel, for teaching job-related skills and a thorough understanding of the organization's policies and procedures, and for mentoring by senior leaders.

The design of leader-development programs varies. Formal learning activities are often necessary for reviewing the basic information about a position, the responsibilities, and the procedures. In addition, prospective leaders who have been assigned to training programs may observe and work with experienced incumbents or may observe how particular functions are carried out in other volunteer organizations. Conferences, workshops, self-directed learning activities such as observation of others in similar positions, and seminars sponsored by other organizations are also important vehicles for the preparation of volunteer leaders. The greater the time available, the greater the opportunity for diverse activities to be incorporated into these programs.

Learning for Personal Growth and Enrichment

When activities are designed to prepare volunteers for new positions, the principal beneficiary of the development process is the organization, which has an opportunity to prepare its future leaders. When activities are designed to promote personal growth, the principal beneficiary is the volunteer, who has an opportunity to grow as a person and to gain a range of skills as the result of the training program. Each organization, as it assesses its staff-development program, must consider the contributions it makes to the personal growth and enrichment of its volunteer staff as a way to recognize their contribution to the organization.

Organizations usually are limited in the ways in which they are able to recognize and reward volunteers explicitly for their service and loyalty. Benefits to volunteers beyond the satisfaction of diligently providing important service are sometimes difficult to identify. Important benefits, however, may be derived from a development program that has as its principal goal enhancing the well-being of volunteers. Fiset, Freeman, Ilsley, and Snow (1987) conclude that volunteers often view their volunteer activity as a form

of self-development and that learning opportunities are an important factor in the satisfaction as well as the retention of volunteers.

Programs that enhance self-esteem, increase knowledge
about some aspect of the program, or share the expertise of a staff
member allow volunteers to grow as persons. Members of the med-
ical staff of a hospital can discuss new treatments for various dis-
eases in lay terms for volunteers. At a monthly gathering for
volunteers in a museum, designated staff members can discuss their
areas of specialization, a new exhibit, or a recent find. Members of
a local teachers' association can meet periodically to discuss financial management, sound investments, and preparation for retire-
ment. Volunteer leaders can be invited to hear prominent speakers
periodically as part of their meetings. In each instance, volunteers
are helped to grow in their knowledge of themselves and of topics
of interest to them.

Characteristics of Effective Programs

Recognition of the important characteristics of learners and the
learning process is integral to the creation of effective volunteer-
development programs. The nature of volunteer learners, what they
bring to the learning experience, the purpose of the learning experience, the climate for learning, and the involvement of volunteers
in planning, implementing, and evaluating the learning program
are all important factors to be considered in the development of
educational programs.

Learners

Any group of volunteers is likely to be heterogeneous, with differences in age, in educational background, in preferred learning style,
and in knowledge of any topic. Some may possess a slight impair-
ment of sight or hearing, or a serious disability. Nevertheless, their
participation as volunteers bespeaks a level of motivation and interest not found in the typical classroom. And, regardless of differences, all volunteers have the capability to learn, although the speed
at which they do so is likely to vary. A successful program will take

these differences into consideration by providing opportunities for individualized as well as group learning experiences.

Learners' Experiences

The heterogeneity of any group of volunteers is evident in the diversity of experiences they bring to a particular job. Dealing with learners' experience is a twofold task: helping them build on experience that is helpful and helping them unlearn experience that is not. Sometimes volunteers' relevant experience must be recognized so they are not retaught what they already know but instead are encouraged to expand their knowledge. Other learners must be helped to analyze experiences that inhibit their ability to perform successfully as volunteers. For example, experiences that lead volunteers to fear or patronize certain groups or individuals may have to be overcome before a volunteer can work with those clients.

In the following illustration, individualized learning activities allow volunteers to develop proficiencies at their own pace.

Volunteers in a church's child-care center range from adolescents to grandparents. Their responsibilities are clearly described in the center's manual, as are the specific tasks at which they are expected to be proficient. Because the volunteers vary greatly in age and in experience working with children, the director of the center has developed a self-teaching module accompanied by a videotape. The printed material gives the rationale for and description of each skill area, and the videotape demonstrates each of the skills. Volunteers may review the instructional materials and practice the required tasks as frequently as necessary according to their own time schedule. When they are able to demonstrate each of the skills for the center director, they are assigned work in the center.

Purpose

All concerned—the leader, the planner, the potential participants, other volunteers, administrators, and paid staff—need to know the purpose of a development program. Writing a clear statement of the goals and objectives forces program leaders to distinguish between knowledge and skills that are optional and those that are necessary for the performance of volunteer tasks. Leaders can then teach volunteers what they need to know to perform a particular task and can use volunteers' time economically. Measurable objectives should be succinctly stated—What precisely will the volunteer know or be able to do as the result of the training?—because adults tend to be motivated to learn what is essential and can be applied immediately. With a clear statement of purpose to guide a leader's preparation as well as a volunteer's expectations, the objectives are likely to become a reality. (See section on Goals and Objectives later in this chapter.)

Learning Climate

In some organizations, members are engaged in self-development and in learning as a means of growth. In others, learning is seen as little more than a way of remedying deficits in individual performance. In an organization where learning is an integral part of the culture, participants are likely to take responsibility for their own learning and help each other to learn through peer teaching and mentoring. Because having opportunities to learn is an important component of volunteer satisfaction, administrators of volunteer programs and other leaders should endeavor to create a climate in which all staff are engaged in self-initiated as well as scheduled efforts to learn.

Volunteer Involvement

Countless opportunities exist in the creation of a volunteer-development program to incorporate the ideas of paid and unpaid staff. Through brainstorming sessions, consultations, and planning committees, many are involved in gathering information and in designing the program. In addition, each step of the program plan, from needs assessment to program presentation, program management, and evaluation, provides an occasion for the staff-development leader to involve knowledgeable and interested volunteers and paid staff and thereby to broaden ownership of the program.

Design of Development Programs

The quality of an educational program depends on appropriate planning activities employed in the proper sequence. Programs designed to facilitate learning among volunteers usually begin with a stated purpose coupled with clearly identified learning needs. Purpose and needs are translated into goals and objectives that provide the foundation for selecting program components and the criteria for program evaluation.

Origins

The development programs of most organizations arise from two sources. The first is the organization's own purpose, its commitment to staff development, and its ongoing program. Out of this organizational context come direction, parameters, and priorities based on the organization's understanding of itself and its mission. Information about an organization's culture is usually available through written policies, declarations of program goals, and mission statements.

The second source of development programs is the needs of volunteers. The organization may identify these needs through survey questionnaires, group discussions, organizational records, critical-incident reports, or reports from administrators. Specific data may be gathered through interviews with volunteers, their supervisors, and their clients; observations of their job performance; or performance reviews. Volunteers are sometimes asked to describe their own performance deficits and to assess their own level of preparedness for a responsibility by identifying the tasks that they are competent to perform. One important source of information is the personal interview, which occurs prior to each assignment; at this time, knowledge and skills as well as attitudes of a potential volunteer may be ascertained to establish the kind of training needed for a particular position.

It is unwise to rely on only a single source of information in developing a program. The use of several sources of information—organizational records, client interviews, and observations of job performance—both confirms and clarifies training needs. Any organization is unlikely through its staff-development program to be able to address all the needs such a comprehensive assessment identifies. Therefore, some ranking must be made on the basis of organizational goals and the severity of the need in order to select those deficits that are to be remedied.

Some organizations use sign-up sheets to probe interest, need, and priorities, as this example illustrates:

> A committee of volunteer tutors at a job-skills center asked all the tutors to identify the most serious problems they faced in their work with adult students. The committee then compiled their responses, combined them into program topics, and prioritized them. Those most frequently listed became topics for training sessions. A bulletin-board advertisement described each session and an accompanying sign-up sheet drew indications from tutors of commitment to participate.

Goals and Objectives

The first step in the creation of a program is the translation of priority learning needs into program goals. A statement of a program goal includes information on the primary focus of the program, the setting in which it will take place, the projected audience, and the time frame. The following is an example of such a statement: "To ensure that all water-safety instructors are up to date in CPR skills, a refresher course in CPR will be offered on Wednesday evenings in March from 7:30 to 8:30 P.M. at the pool." The statement is useful for publicity, budgeting, securing facilities and other resources, and program design. The development of a program goal forces the planner to consider the best way to deliver the program. Which volunteers need the program? What location is convenient for them? When are they available? Should the learning activity be held during their volunteer time or should it be a discrete event?

The next step is the development of learning objectives.

These are specific descriptions of what the trainee will know, believe, or be able to do as the result of the staff-development experience. For example:

A person who has completed the refresher course in CPR will be able to:

- describe situations where CPR might appropriately be used
- describe the two components of CPR
- demonstrate each component
- perform CPR correctly using the resuscitation dummy

Objectives that describe behaviors, using verbs such as *list, explain, demonstrate,* or *perform,* are more clearly understood and their outcomes are more easily assessed than are those that describe unobservable processes, such as *understand* or *appreciate.*

Techniques

The following key concepts govern the selection of training techniques: first, the techniques should be appropriate for achieving the objective; second, the techniques should be feasible, given the size and characteristics of the group and the physical setting and time available; third, the techniques should provide for active participation by the volunteer trainee; and, fourth, the techniques should provide for some variety. Furthermore, the setting in which the knowledge or skill is practiced, insofar as possible, should resemble the setting in which the volunteer will work.

Techniques appropriate for staff-development programs that have as their purpose imparting knowledge include lectures, interviews, films, slides, audiotapes and videotapes, colloquia, interrogator panels, panel discussions, symposia, debates, and dramatic presentations. These techniques may be supplemented through the use of buzz groups, group discussions, huddle groups, question periods, reaction panels, and other follow-up techniques.

Techniques appropriate for teaching a skill or new behavior

include case study, coaching, demonstration, structured experience, simulation, and a teaching/learning team. Supplementary follow-up techniques include application projects, drills, and practice sessions.

Techniques appropriate for assisting volunteers to change their attitudes, values, opinions, or feelings include structured experiences and exercises, field trips, games, group discussions, role playing, sensitivity groups, simulations, skits, and values-clarification exercises. These techniques require follow-up programs for discussing and processing the experience. (For additional information on training techniques, see Robinson, 1983.)

All these techniques may be supplemented by using printed materials, worksheets, overhead transparencies, chalkboards, and flip charts. In fact, it is generally believed that persons who receive stimuli through more than one sense—seeing and hearing, for example—are more likely to retain what they learn than are those stimulated through only one sense.

Adapting Standardized Programs

Many organizations involving volunteers are connected with similar organizations through coalitions and networks or are related structurally to similar units across the country. In this case, volunteer responsibilities, orientation to the program, and preparation for a particular job are frequently standardized. Sometimes the use of national or regional training materials is mandated; other times the material is available for use by a local unit.

When high-quality training material is available from a national organization, certain advantages are derived from its use: the need to create program materials is eliminated, local resources are conserved, and the organization is able to provide training consistent with the direction of the national organization. Furthermore, national organizations often provide technical assistance and support to those who use the materials. In some cases, national organizations train local training staff.

At the same time, care must be exercised to adapt nationally developed materials to local use and to give them enough local flavor so that they reflect the goals of the local organization. The reasons excellent materials fail are generally preventable: local staff members are not trained in their use, the local level of performance and proficiency differs from the national level and adjustments are not made, and local emphases are not incorporated into the program.

Evaluation

Information vital to every planner is the degree to which a particular program achieves its objectives. That information comes from various sources: participants, supervisors, clients, and administrators. Successful program planners actively gather such information through surveys, interviews, conversations, observations, and organizational records to document the outcomes and to improve the quality of their programs. Evaluation may probe volunteers' reactions to training, differences in volunteer performance, or differences in the organization's ability to perform its mission. Various aspects of program evaluation are discussed in Chapter Eight.

Management

Organizations and agencies are assisted in the execution of staff-development programs when they have a written statement of volunteer-development policies and procedures, of the content of the training program for each position, and of the title of the person responsible for performing the training. Such a statement clarifies responsibility and assists all involved in the staff-development effort.

In addition, decisions need to be made concerning the make-up of the group to be trained, activities other than education that will be included, the setting in which the learning activity will occur, and the continuity of staff-development events. Decisions about group makeup are based on the program goals and objectives. Is this event designed for all volunteers or for volunteers and paid staff, or is it designed for a particular subunit? Will volunteers whose work is highly individual or performed at a remote site be included?

Decisions about whom to include, in turn, influence decisions about activities, other than educational ones, to be offered. Would it be useful to include opportunities for recognition and fellowship? If many people are involved, will opportunities for breaking into subunits be available? If only a subunit is involved, will there be recognition that the subunit is an important part of a larger agency?

Decisions about the setting for training are based on the size of the group, whether the staff-development activity occurs simultaneously with volunteer work or at a different time, and whether the event includes time for fellowship, socialization, and recognition. Transportation, parking, and security are often also important considerations.

An effective staff-development program is a continuing one, provided on a regular basis (monthly, quarterly, semiannually), with clear expectations for volunteer participation. Training done on an ad hoc basis, prompted by crises or problems, indicates uncertainty about the need for or content of the training. When training is scheduled over the long term, it appears as an important part of the ongoing life of the organization.

Leaders of Training Programs

The question Who should do the training? has many answers, each with its own potentially positive consequences. In selecting leaders for staff-development programs, those responsible should consider both the skills and the abilities of the individuals as well as other benefits that may accrue to an organization.

Administrator of Volunteer Programs

The task of orienting volunteers to an organization or preparing them for a specific responsibility typically is the responsibility of the administrator of volunteer programs. In a centralized volunteer program, this person also performs such important ancillary functions as keeping records of participation, scheduling programs, and recognizing both leaders and trainees. Nevertheless, the administrator's responsibility for staff development does not preclude the involvement of others in this activity.

Volunteers

Using volunteers as trainers is an excellent way to provide experienced volunteers with opportunities for advanced responsibility within an organization and at the same time to increase the credibility of the training because the trainer, like the trainee, is a volunteer.

Paid Staff

Paid staff within an organization possess considerable expertise about its program and job responsibilities, making them logical choices for leadership in the staff-development program. Because they also are frequently in a position to supervise volunteers, assigning them training responsibilities enables them to play a major role in the preparation of the volunteers with whom they work. In addition, using paid staff in this way has the potential for improving volunteer/paid-staff relations. Kane-Williams, Salisbury, and Benson (1989, p. 482) describe a national health-maintenance program for older Americans in which the training was conducted by teams of health professionals and lay volunteers, many of whom had teaching experience in a non–health-related area. The team approach reduced work loads, combined different areas of expertise, introduced variety, and resulted in collaborative efforts that had a positive impact on the program in general.

Organization Administrators

Several advantages accrue from using administrators in the training of volunteers. First, it conveys the impression to the volunteer trainees that they are of importance to the organization. Second, an administrator may be able to bring an organizational perspective to a training session that is different from the perspective of other staff persons. And, third, involving administrators in training familiarizes them with the volunteer program and acquaints them with members of the volunteer corps.

Human Resource Development Department

Organizations large enough to have a separate unit responsible for human resource development may wish to involve these professional trainers in volunteer-development programs. Human resource development departments often have significant resources— personnel, materials, equipment, and knowledge about instructional technology—to contribute to staff-development efforts.

Leaders from Outside the Organization

Noted experts have much to contribute to the staff-development program of an organization and to the personal development of volunteers. Organizations with limited budgets for staff development may want to invite professionals and volunteers from similar organizations to serve as volunteer-development leaders on a reciprocal basis.

Conclusion

The most effective staff-development programs have two components. The first is a well-planned educational program for volunteers and paid staff that demonstrates that the organization takes its mission and its personnel resources seriously. An effective training program provides for the development of volunteers, keeping in focus the organization's goals. When proficiency in carrying out the organization's mission is held forth as the standard, volunteers and paid staff are proud to be associated with the cause.

The second component is an organizational climate that recognizes the motivation of volunteers both to serve and to learn. In an organization that assumes that volunteers will bear some responsibility for their own learning, promotes self-directed learning, and encourages volunteers to analyze and reflect on their own experience as an important learning procedure, the potential for persons to improve their proficiency and increase their value to the organization on their own initiative is limitless.

7

Supervising Volunteers to Strengthen Performance and Retention

A lthough volunteers may participate in the same orientation and training programs, diverse motives, interests, needs, and skills are reflected in their individual performance. The diversity frequently found in groups of volunteers can be seen in the following illustration:

> A team of five to seven volunteers is required on a daily basis to operate the various sections of the interactive, discovery-learning exhibits of a children's museum. On any day, the volunteer administrator is faced with the task of providing supervision to a diverse group of volunteers: a retired elementary school-teacher, a retired banker, a disabled older adult whose doctor had recommended volunteer work to combat depression, a homemaker exploring career options, two high school students from a community-service class, and a university student working toward a career as an exhibit designer.

What skills are required of the supervisor if this diverse group is to work as a cohesive team? What attitudes does the supervisor need in order to enhance the personal growth and satisfaction of each of these volunteers? How does the supervisor create a meaningful experience for each volunteer and at the same time ensure that organizational goals are met? How can consistent standards of performance be maintained?

Although organizations design supervisory systems to meet the unique needs for support and guidance of their volunteer staff, each organization should be prepared to provide adequate volunteer orientation and on-the-job training; clearly communicated minimum standards of performance; access to the supervisor as needed; documentation systems that record volunteer hours and activities; annual (at a minimum) individual performance reviews; and staff readiness for volunteer participation, including a training program for supervisors of volunteers.

Who Supervises?

Volunteers evolve in their respective roles through their interactions with each other and, more significantly, through their interactions with their supervisor. In a study of volunteer satisfaction, Gidron (1983) found that adequate supervision and assistance from supervisory staff were important determinants of individuals' satisfaction with their volunteer experience. Other research on volunteers' attitudes toward supervisors (Colomy, Chen, and Andrews, 1987) indicates that the competence of the immediate supervisor and the guidance and support provided by the supervisor ranked fourth and fifth out of twenty factors important to volunteers' effectiveness.

Because the quality of the relationship between volunteer and supervisor is so critical, the question of who supervises is vitally important to the success of the volunteer program. Equally essential is the allocation of adequate resources for the supervision of volunteer efforts: supervisory costs are likely to be the highest of all those associated with the management of the volunteer program.

In most centralized programs, where the main functions of the organization are performed by volunteers, the volunteer administrator serves as the supervisor of all volunteer staff. However, it should be noted that the time-consuming nature of this responsibility may prevent further development of the volunteer program as a whole. In decentralized organizations, where volunteers are placed in various ongoing units, the volunteer administrator shares supervisory responsibility with other paid staff or delegates it completely.

After placement, the classroom teacher, ward supervisor, program manager, or curator provides direct supervision of the volunteer on a day-to-day basis.

The following case illustrates how the supervisory needs of volunteers in a decentralized program were met:

> In a probation program designed to prevent recidivism, volunteers requested clinical supervision. Although their training had prepared them to work with probationers and their families, they recognized that the complex needs of the families required advanced training. Although the program's budget did not include funds for a highly skilled clinical consultant, the volunteer administrator was able to recruit a retired social worker with experience in the area of probations. He provided clinical supervision and support to the volunteers, while the volunteer administrator continued to function as the program manager by recruiting volunteers, arranging for monthly meetings, and supervising volunteers in the nonclinical facets of the program.

In some organizations, volunteers provide supervision for other volunteers through the use of a career ladder that advances volunteers to supervisory positions. According to Ellis (1991), "Volunteers make excellent mid-level supervisors of other volunteers. Using them encourages a team approach. . . . " In addition to minimizing the time and expense of involving paid staff in the supervision of volunteers, use of this option is a way to promote and recognize experienced volunteers. The volunteer administrator or other paid staff member provides the training, advice, and ongoing support needed by these unpaid supervisors of volunteers.

Requirements for Supervisory Positions

Adequate Training

Wilson states that volunteer/paid-staff relations are the foremost problem in volunteerism (1981) and that a major challenge in the voluntary sector is preparing paid staff to work effectively with volunteers (1984). As Wilson points out, volunteers are frequently managed or supervised by persons who have no training in how to work with volunteers.

Because the success of the volunteer program relies to a great degree on the supervisory abilities of staff, the training of supervisory staff is critical. The first need to be addressed in this training is the need to recognize and appreciate the unique characteristics of volunteer staff. Volunteers are not dependent on the organization for pay, have sources of motivation different from those of paid staff, gain different benefits, and work part-time instead of full-time. They require supervisors who recognize these characteristics. Such supervisors communicate respect for the volunteer as a colleague working to achieve an organization's mission.

Topics that may be incorporated into a training program in order to increase staff readiness to supervise volunteers include these:

- How to involve volunteers effectively
- How to enhance the value of volunteers to a program and to a paid employee
- How to include volunteers in program planning and decision making
- How to evaluate volunteer performance
- How to provide performance feedback to volunteers
- How to hold volunteers accountable for job performance
- How to help volunteers avoid burnout
- How to create a climate in which volunteers will be most productive
- How to build teams that include both volunteers and paid employees

The second need to be addressed in the training of supervisory staff is the need to deal effectively with problems involving volunteers. Organizations should have clear and publicly stated policies concerning the professional behavior of all staff. Supervisors of volunteers on occasion must respond to situations where volunteers do not act accordingly: absenteeism, tardiness, failure to perform tasks listed in a job description, and breech of confidentiality are some of the problems most commonly faced.

Positive Attitudes

The interest and willingness of supervisory staff to provide the guidance and support needed by volunteers are requirements as critical as a training program.

> A manufacturing company with an employee volunteer program approached the executive director of a residential treatment center for emotionally disturbed boys about the possibility of volunteers' organizing weekend recreational activities for the boys. The executive director shared the idea at his next staff meeting. The professional social-work staff employed on weekends replied that they were already required to supervise relatively inexperienced paraprofessional child-care workers; they rejected the added burden of supervising volunteers who would not know how to deal with emotionally disturbed boys.

In this example, the lack of willingness of paid staff to provide the guidance and support that would enable volunteer participation was based on their perceptions of volunteers' abilities and the degree of supervision they would require.

In many other situations also, the way supervisors operate is necessarily influenced by their perceptions of those they supervise. McGregor's "Theory X-Theory Y" (1966) can be used to describe the differences in perception between staff members who trust volunteers and those who do not. According to McGregor, supervisory style is based on assumptions about human nature and human motivation. His theory X supervisors assume that people prefer not be self-directed, are not interested in assuming responsibility, and want safety above all. They also see people as being motivated by money, fringe benefits, and the threat of punishment. Paid staff with this orientation will want to create an environment that is structured and controlled. These supervisors are likely to be ineffective with the majority of volunteers because often volunteers' safety needs have been met, and their social, esteem, and self-actualization needs are dominant.

McGregor's Theory Y supervisors assume that people are self-directed, creative, and internally motivated. In their work with volunteers they create opportunities, release potential, remove obstacles, encourage growth, and provide guidance. They demonstrate their trust in volunteers by creating an environment that allows a high degree of individuality and volunteer involvement in planning and problem solving.

Paid staff who trust volunteers can be easily identified. They treat volunteers as equals, offer volunteers opportunities to take the initiative, and invite volunteers to attend regular staff meetings to offer opinions about organizational goals, programs, policies, and procedures. They also allow volunteers a high degree of self-sufficiency in the work environment. They enthusiastically examine the work of the organization to determine areas in which volunteer contributions will be most beneficial.

Although it is important to identify staff who mistrust volunteers, it is also important, and often more difficult, to identify staff who merely tolerate them. Their lack of enthusiasm for the participation of volunteers is communicated via subtle, negative messages, such as halfhearted greetings, lukewarm expressions of appreciation, "forgetting" to invite volunteers to staff meetings, and, in general, consistently giving minimal attention to the needs of volunteers. The impact of supervision of this nature becomes apparent in the increasing unreliability of formerly reliable volunteers and in the eventual departure of long-term volunteers from the organization.

Just as volunteer administrators need to develop skill in the selection of volunteer staff, they also need to develop skill in assessing the ability of paid staff and volunteers to serve as supervisors. An organization whose supervisors welcome the participation of volunteers will have a strong foundation for healthy volunteer/paid-staff relationships and a promising future in meeting organizational goals.

Well-Developed Supervisory Skills

In addition to being well trained and having positive attitudes toward volunteers, supervisors must be able to create a supportive environment, employ team-building techniques, delegate responsibility, communicate clearly and appropriately, provide feedback, appraise volunteer performance, and either correct performance problems or take disciplinary action. Development of supervisory skills in these areas results in improved volunteer/paid-staff relations and enhanced volunteer performance.

Creating a Supportive Environment. The American Management Association (Gardner, 1980) emphasizes two elements of a supportive environment: training and good work conditions. Each contributes to enhanced worker performance and satisfaction. Training gives workers a clear understanding of job assignments, information about standards and expected levels of performance, and instruction in how to do the job. When work conditions are good, obstacles to doing a job are eliminated, adequate resources are provided, and conditions harmful to performance are corrected.

The following case shows how an organization dealt with training and work-condition challenges:

A national professional association with over eighty thousand members was organized into a number of regions, each composed of ten to fifteen smaller local units called sections. Volunteer regional directors supplied training, support, and resources to volunteer section leaders. Each regional director conducted an annual orientation and training session for new section leaders and was available for consultation by telephone as needed. However, the quality of the training materials was inconsistent because regional directors developed their own resources. Recognizing the potential negative impact of this inconsistency on section leaders and ultimately on the organization's ability to retain members, supervisory staff at the national office compiled the best of the regional training

materials into a resource packet and distributed it to
all regional directors and section leaders.

The creation and maintenance of training programs and
work conditions that help to guide and support volunteers are essential supervisory functions. Macduff (1991) refers to this function
as providing the "sustenance" that preserves the involvement and
motivation of volunteers and enables optimal performance. She
suggests that sustenance is particularly important for short-term
volunteers. Ilsley (1990) suggests that when the right volunteer is in
the right job, the personal involvement of the supervisor is the extra
element needed to ensure high-quality performance. He encourages
supervisors to let volunteers know they are cared about as individuals in addition to being appreciated for their contributions of time
and talent to the organization.

In addition to sustenance, most volunteers need self-
determination in order to perform at their best. Supervisors can
provide an essential foundation for self-determination by supporting autonomy, providing noncontrolling, positive feedback, and
acknowledging volunteers' perspectives. Deci, Connell, and Ryan
(1981) found that volunteers' performance and satisfaction were
highest when supervisors promoted and supported the higher-order
need for self-determination by encouraging personal initiative. In
addition, supervisory styles that permit flexibility in job performance are positively associated with high quality of work life and
organizational effectiveness (Likert, 1961; Herzberg, 1966). How a
supervisor handles limits, choices, and decision making influences
the extent to which volunteers find the environment conducive to
self-determination.

Team Building. Productive volunteer/paid-staff relationships center on teams, in which paid and volunteer staff serve the organization together in order to accomplish goals. Each has a sense of
ownership of the organization and values the other's contributions.
All positions are considered important for the attainment of organizational goals, and volunteers are involved at all levels of planning and decision making.

Clear lines of authority continue to exist in a team approach;

the work of volunteer staff is directly supervised by either another volunteer or a paid staff member of the organization. In a team approach, the supervisor provides "coaching" (Macduff, 1986), offering ongoing guidance to volunteers by continually providing relevant information on effective ways to do the job and suggesting steps for improvement.

Reilly and Jones (1974) identify several important elements that must be present for a group to work as a team: a reason to work together, a need for the others' experience, a commitment to the idea that working together leads to effective results, and accountability as a functioning group within a larger organizational context.

Hersey and Blanchard (1982) affirm that teams can be more effective when they purposely comprise individuals with diverse values, styles, and skills rather than individuals who are similar. Compatibility of team members is not dependent on similarity but on establishing common goals and objectives. Hersey and Blanchard encourage building work teams in which new recruits complement rather than replicate current members. In addition, teams need an atmosphere that allows open dialogue and a certain amount of open expression of differing points of view. The following case illustrates how a volunteer leader encouraged team building:

> A group of leaders of an organization for girls was involved in the planning and management of a district, a group of fifteen different troops consisting of girls aged six to eighteen from varying racial and ethnic groups and of differing economic status. The chairperson of the district, who was in her second year of office, felt she could enhance working relationships by improving the integration of new and experienced leaders, building on the strengths of each leader, and facilitating the establishment of group goals and priorities so that each leader would feel that the needs of her particular troop were addressed.
>
> The chairperson was assisted by a volunteer management consultant, who facilitated a day-long retreat for the leaders in which they shared their mo-

tivations for becoming troop leaders, identified their different leadership styles, and discussed their priorities. As a group, they agreed to make decisions by consensus rather than by the more traditional system of majority rule, and they made the commitment to strive to create a year-long series of activities that would meet the diverse needs and interests of the girls they served.

Delegating Responsibility. Developing the ability of others to assume responsibility is a key task of supervisors, and skill in effective delegation is central to the supervisory function. Although supervisors are ultimately responsible for completion of the tasks assigned to their group, delegating to others the authority to perform activities and the responsibility for their successful completion is essential.

The following case describes the benefits of effective delegation skills:

A large urban church had just hired its first paid volunteer administrator to be in charge of a program to serve a nightly meal to homeless individuals and families. Initially, she recruited, trained, scheduled, and supervised the volunteer staff. In addition, she ordered the food, met the delivery van, stocked the pantry, set the tables, greeted guests, and did a great deal of clean-up because she had to stay late to turn off the lights and lock up. The volunteers expressed concern about her ability to continue handling such a work load and encouraged her to delegate increased responsibility to them.

They suggested that their jobs be enlarged to include her additional duties and that they work in teams of two and be assigned a different set of weekly "chores" in addition to preparing and serving the meals. The volunteers enjoyed the diversity of duties and the opportunity to get to know one another better by working in teams. The volunteer administrator was

able to work three or four nights each week rather
than seven and could go home early by assigning volunteers to close the church.

Delegation benefits supervisors by relieving the pressure and stress
associated with large work loads and by allowing them time to
concentrate on supervisory responsibilities. Delegation benefits subordinates by enhancing their self-esteem, fostering participation
and initiative, providing job enrichment, and preparing them for
advanced responsibility.

The Institute for Financial Education (1988) suggests a six-
step approach to effective delegation: choose the right task, choose
the right person to do it, give clear instructions, turn the task over
to the worker but stay in contact, give authority, and review results
with the worker.

Direct oversight of activities may not be possible because of
the time and place of a volunteer's assignment. These conditions
make it especially important that the assignment clearly specify
results, that the volunteer's authority be well-defined, that the supervisor be readily available for consultation and problem solving,
and that meetings with the volunteer be scheduled on a regular
basis.

Communicating Effectively. Communication that is competent and
appropriate can have a healthy, positive effect on the climate and
productivity of an organization. Effective verbal and written communication skills are essential in all facets of the administration of
volunteer efforts, but they are particularly vital in the supervisory
role. The effective articulation of organizational goals, the skillful
introduction of change, the clarification of tasks and standards of
performance, the delegation of responsibility, team building, and
the provision of instruction and feedback all require highly developed communication skills.

Communication is successful only when accurate, mutual understanding is achieved on the part of sender and receiver. A good
communicator checks out the degree to which the intended message
is received and comprehended. It is not necessary that the two parties
agree but rather that they understand the message.

The supervisor is the key person in the communication chain of the organization. Some have characterized the role of the supervisor as that of linking an organization's middle and upper management with their direct-service personnel. As a link, the supervisor communicates on behalf of organizational leaders to volunteers engaged as service providers and communicates on behalf of volunteers to the organization's managers and leaders.

Listening skills are especially important for supervisors so that they can obtain the most accurate understanding of information given to them by volunteers as well as by other members of the organization. The Institute for Financial Education (1988) defines listening as the "process of translating a spoken message into an understood concept." Listening involves hearing, as the ear perceives sounds; comprehending, as the sounds convey meaning; remembering, as the mind retains the message; and responding. Good listening skills can enable supervisors to improve their sensitivity to workers' feelings and receive early warning of potential problems.

A technique termed *active listening* requires elimination of all distractions and complete focus on the speaker. Active listeners have face-to-face contact with the speaker, withhold judgment, remain quiet until the speaker has completed the message, and then respond. During the course of listening, the listener mentally organizes the speaker's message and verifies it through paraphrasing. George (1982) adds that it is important to be aware of and to minimize the effect of one's biases and to work hard to understand difficult messages from the speaker's point of view.

One-way communication is faster than two-way communication and is more effectively used if the appearance of efficiency is a priority. However, two-way communication, in which both the sender and the receiver of messages are active participants, is usually more accurate. Because words mean different things to different people, the advantage of the two-way message is that the receiver can question the sender about meaning and point out additional perspectives on the issue at hand as well as any mistakes or oversights.

Two-way communication accompanies a consultative supervisory style, in which subordinates participate in the planning and implementation of tasks and the solution of problems. Morale is high because workers' ideas are heard and valued. Two-way communication is essential for team building. The use of such communication techniques is the most effective way for supervisors to introduce change. When workers are involved in problem solving and when one-on-one discussions are held with those individuals who are affected, the possibility of worker acceptance and support of change is enhanced.

Providing Feedback. Communication skills are also important in providing feedback about performance.

> A volunteer administrator who manages over one hundred crisis-line volunteers schedules them in pairs, matching experienced phone counselors with newly trained volunteers. Experienced volunteers provide new recruits with verbal feedback on their performance and assist them if a call becomes too difficult for them. The experienced volunteers also complete an observation form that the volunteer administrator reads the next day, assessing the strengths of the new volunteer and expressing any concerns about the volunteer's method of handling crisis calls.

Feedback always describes performance in behavioral rather than personal terms; it is descriptive rather than judgmental. For example, feedback focuses on the number of clients served or the number of times the volunteer was absent rather than on the motivation of the volunteer. On a regular basis, the supervisor can provide informal feedback to each volunteer, describing performance as progress toward goals; it is also important to assess how the team has done and how "we" can improve. Providing feedback on performance is a supervisory skill that, if handled properly, can stimulate improved performance and serve as a form of volunteer recognition.

Appraising Performance. The trend has been to develop volunteer programs based to a significant degree on the traditional workplace

model, including the use of performance reviews. Although informal feedback is essential on a regular basis, formal feedback to
volunteers in the form of individual performance appraisals is also
an important part of a well-developed volunteer program. These
appraisals also provide an opportunity to solicit feedback from volunteers about their experience, the volunteer program, and the organization.

The research of Colomy, Chen, and Andrews (1987) indicates
that because volunteers are providing a gift of their time and talents
for which they are not being remunerated, they expect to be treated
in a manner significantly different from the typical employee. Their
findings suggest that respect for and recognition of volunteers' non-
paid status must be inherent in the way they are assessed. The role
of the volunteer administrator is to establish an approach to the
appraisal of performance that is acceptable to volunteers yet allows
the organization to set and control performance standards.

According to English (1991) the appraisal should be based on
predetermined and clearly communicated performance standards.
Because a formal appraisal is a specific event in an ongoing process
of feedback and supervision, it should introduce no surprises. Too
frequently, however, volunteers do not know what is expected of
them, their performance is infrequently and ineffectively assessed,
and their rewards are not directly tied to performance. English advocates use of "Rational Performance Management," in which individuals' responsibilities support organizational goals within a
performance-focused organizational culture. Performance can then
be measured and assessed on the basis of those responsibilities and
goals. English warns supervisors against making sweeping or over-
generalized appraisals and suggests that appraisals be based on per-
tinent and specific criteria that can be judged and explained. He
also calls for the evaluation of traits as well as skills because a
volunteer's attitudes, communication style, leadership activities,
and appearance are all qualities critical to successful performance.

On the basis of their research on the role of supervisors'
memories in appraising performance, DeNisi, Robbins, and Cafferty (1989) recommend use of a diary to record information that
might otherwise be forgotten. The diary is especially helpful when
there are competing demands for supervisors' time and attention.

Giles and Mossholder (1990) suggest that how the supervisor behaves in a review session influences a subordinate's satisfaction with it. Volunteers' satisfaction with performance appraisals is critical to their job satisfaction and productivity; if poorly done, the appraisal can seriously impair job performance. Fulmer and Franklin (1982) offer these guidelines for supervisors in the appraisal interview:

1. Use clear communication regarding the performance to be discussed. This requires that the organization begin its involvement of volunteers with clear job descriptions and expectations for minimum standards of performance.
2. Focus on progress toward specific behavioral or performance goals rather than generalized performance.
3. Give praise for strong and/or improved performance. . . .
4. Use a team problem-solving approach.
5. Discuss the need for improvement and provide concrete suggestions, training, and support to enable the volunteer to achieve success.
6. Appraise the job performance, not the person.

Other techniques for formal performance appraisal include self-assessment and peer review. Gaston (1989, p. 29) suggests that self-assessment "is probably the least threatening way to begin, especially if it is linked to program evaluation so that volunteers see the purpose as growth and development rather than judgment or criticism." In self-assessment, volunteers are provided with a questionnaire to which they respond by scoring themselves on a number of factors related to their performance. Self-assessment may simply be a reexamination of the volunteer job description, focusing on the degree to which volunteers have fulfilled their time commitment and performed their duties, or self-assessment can focus on performance strengths and weaknesses by having volunteers reflect on how they handled particular situations or tasks, the degree to which they met both personal and organizational goals, and the skill areas in which they would like to improve. A self-assessment question-naire also may include a section in which volunteers commit to another period of time in the same position, express interest in a change of position within the organization, or release themselves from their involvement.

Peer review is another valid performance-appraisal option.

> An older-adult peer-counseling program involved vol-unteers age fifty-five and above as facilitators of dis-cussion groups for other older adults. On an annual basis, each volunteer observed at least two groups led by peers and provided them with written feedback. Feedback focused on the strengths observed, the par-ticipants' response to the facilitator, ways in which the volunteer could improve the sessions, and what ob-servers learned that they could replicate in their own sessions.

Peer review offers volunteers the opportunity to learn from each other. They see each other as resources and gain insights into dif-ferent styles of working toward the same goals. Volunteer admin-istrators who chose to integrate peer review into their performance-appraisal system need also to provide orientation to volunteers on ways to provide feedback to peers in helpful, nonjudgmental, and, in the case of negative feedback, constructive ways.

Gaston (1989) describes a three-step process for gradually in-troducing performance evaluation into a long-standing volunteer program. The following case illustrates this process:

> A telephone crisis-counseling program had been oper-ated as an all-volunteer effort for many years. When an executive director was hired and began to introduce performance reviews, many long-time volunteers felt threatened. Their response was, "We've been doing just fine without report cards." The board of directors, however, supported making evaluation part of the pro-gram and formed a committee to work with the new executive director to develop a sensitive and gradual

process for assessing volunteer performance. The committee created a three-step program that was introduced over the next three years: (1) a self-assessment, in
which each volunteer was asked to rate his or her handling of various kinds and aspects of calls; (2) a peer
evaluation, in which each volunteer was asked to cri-
tique another volunteer's performance; and (3) an evaluation instrument, in which volunteers were asked to
review an audiotaped simulated crisis call and reflect
on the strengths and weaknesses of the counselor.

*Correcting Performance Problems and Taking Disciplinary Ac-
tion.* The task of the supervisor faced with poor performance is to
identify reasons for it in order to make appropriate corrections.
Dugan (1989) proposes that this diagnostic phase be interactive and
that the supervisor work with the volunteer to discover and interpret
reasons for nonattainment of goals and to plan for ways to improve
performance. Through these discussions the supervisor can assess
whether the performance problem arises from characteristics of the
individual, such as level of effort or ability; characteristics of the
situation, such as task difficulty or obstacles; or some combination
of these characteristics. Then, the supervisor and the volunteer must
work together to identify adjustments needed to bring about improvement on the part of both the volunteer and the organization.

On occasion, however, disciplinary action may be needed to
correct a situation in which a volunteer's behavior departs from an
organization's policy or is detrimental to the volunteer program and
the organization. Volunteers must first receive information on organizational policies, actions that would be defined as misconduct,
and the consequences. Eckles, Carmichael, and Sarchet (1983)
recommend a first warning that clearly communicates the consequences of a second incident. If a second incident occurs, disciplinary action should be immediate, consistent, and impersonal, as in
the following example:

Seven teen volunteers from a high school community-
service class worked together at a concession stand to
raise funds for a health organization. Each was as-

signed to a specific post and set of responsibilities. One teen had a tendency to lose interest in his assignment and to visit with his female classmates at their posts. His socialization needs obviously outweighed his need to do well in the class by fulfilling his responsibility. At first, the supervisor of the concession stand patiently reiterated the reasons it was important for the teen to remain at his assigned post. After several of the other volunteers complained about the teen's lack of responsibility, the supervisor contacted the volunteer administrator, who in turn talked with both the teen and the teacher, reconfirmed expectations, and allowed the young man another chance. When the volunteer continued to be disruptive, he was dismissed.

Releasing a volunteer from a position is one of the most difficult tasks in volunteer administration. To prevent negative and unfortunate situations from developing, it is necessary to have a sound system of recruitment, screening, selection, and orientation. Poor performance on the part of one volunteer can damage a volunteer program in a number of ways:

1. Paid staff who may be negative or ambivalent about involving volunteers in the work of the organization feel their position is justified.
2. Other volunteers who take professional pride in their efforts may be less committed if an organization fails to maintain standards of behavior and performance for all.
3. Positive volunteer/paid-staff relations may be threatened as staff members who were once open to designing positions for volunteers lose some of their enthusiasm.
4. The quality of service to the clients or customers of the organization is diminished by even one poor performer.

Conclusion

The guidance and support an organization provides to its volunteer staff are essential to their successful performance and to the achievement of organizational goals. Organizations that allocate resources to volunteer supervision are assured a significant return on their investment because volunteer retention, customer satisfaction, and volunteer/paid-staff relations are enhanced as a result.

At times it may be appropriate for the volunteer administrator to serve as the direct supervisor of volunteers; in other cases, supervision may be delegated to either paid or unpaid staff. However, the volunteer administrator must always ensure that supervisory staff receive adequate training for the role, that performance expectations are clearly communicated to volunteers, and that a performance-appraisal system is in place.

Short-term volunteers may not require formal performance reviews; a thank-you note with information on how they helped the group or organization make progress toward a goal is adequate feedback. Longer-term volunteers who have a regular, ongoing position can benefit from a performance-review process, whether in the form of self-evaluation, peer review, or supervisor feedback.

8

Evaluating Volunteer Efforts

Volunteer administrators are continually faced with the need to demonstrate the value of their programs. Potential funding sources need evidence of program outcomes to decide on allocation commitments; agency executives need data to support decisions to continue a program; and current and potential volunteers want to know that their efforts produce identifiable results. Findings derived from program evaluations not only contribute to important funding, programming, and staffing decisions but also provide the foundation for planning future directions. Because programs involving volunteers must compete for resources in the community as well as within the organization, program evaluation has become an indispensable tool of the volunteer administrator for demonstrating program quality and accountability in the use of resources and for gaining the support of organizational leaders, external funders, and program participants themselves.

Another important use of the findings is in improving the quality of a particular program. Examination of strengths and weaknesses provides the basis for continuing certain aspects of a program and making changes in others. Attention and effort devoted to evaluation communicate to funders, administrators, volunteers, and clients that an organization cares enough about its programs to be willing to scrutinize them in order to assure their quality.

Regardless of the purpose for examining a program, most evaluations focus on effectiveness and efficiency. A study of effectiveness questions the degree to which program goals are achieved and the degree to which identified needs are met. According to Gamm and Kassab (1983, p. 25), "Effectiveness is concerned chiefly with the quality or impact of the program's output, that is, with the relationship between outputs and outcomes." Questions about the effectiveness of a particular service include: How many clients are served and what is the quality of that service (output)? What are the consequences of that service to the clients or the community (outcomes)? And how does that service aid the organization in fulfilling its mission?

A study of efficiency examines the use of resources: usually an efficiency measure compares the cost to the organization of providing volunteer services with the estimated value to clients of the services provided. An efficiency measure may provide a basis on which to compare the respective costs of alternative strategies for service delivery; for example, an organization might compare the costs and benefits of providing a service using volunteers with the costs and benefits of providing the same service using paid staff. Other efficiency studies consider ways to increase the quality or quantity of volunteer service without increasing volunteer time and organizational costs.

What to Evaluate

An evaluation can examine one of three aspects of a program—its process, its results, or its broad impact—or any combination of these elements.

Process

Organizational process comprises the day-to-day operation of a program, how the program functions. A process evaluation of a volunteer program examines the tasks volunteers perform, the skills and abilities they bring to their jobs, their position guides, their job performance, their satisfaction with the program, the amount of time they contribute, their retention, and the cost of paid staff required to support their efforts. Allen (1987, p. 261) proposes that process evaluations of client-focused programs also include "assessment of clients' perceptions of volunteers [and] periodic progress reports prepared by volunteers describing their activities with clients."

A process evaluation also examines the coordination and administration of a program, the assignment of volunteer tasks, the adequacy of supervision, the effectiveness of training, the level of staff and budgetary support available, and performance expectations. It reviews lines of communication and accountability and identifies potential sources of internal conflict. Langer (1987) also recommends monitoring the total resources devoted to a particular project to ensure that the amount is consistent with the priority assigned to that project within the organization.

Organizations and agencies may find examination of all of these elements impossible because of time and budget constraints. Careful planning for a process evaluation requires identifying those elements judged to be important and supplying a rationale for their inclusion.

Results

Evaluation of results looks at the direct consequences or outputs of a program, the products and services that a program provides. Using such information as the number of clients served, the amount of service provided, or the amount of money raised, it studies any direct results of the efforts of a volunteer program. For example, a results evaluation might note the number of adult students tutored in a literacy program, the improvement each showed in reading skill, and the number who completed the program and obtained their high school equivalency diploma.

Other measures of results include the percentage of participants who lowered their blood pressure, reported increased ability to deal with anger or stress, raised their educational achievement levels, remained pregnancy-free during their teen years, increased involvement in their children's education, or recruited at least one new member for the organization.

The evaluation of results is based on the organization's goals and objectives—that is, its projection of the direct consequences of a program. An organization establishes its evaluation criteria in clearly written, measurable objectives.

Impact

Impact evaluation measures the broad consequences of a program, such as how the lives of clients have improved or how the health of a community has changed or how the organization has been helped in achieving its mission. Impact evaluation usually examines the degree to which the overall needs a program was designed to address have in fact been alleviated. For example, a water-safety program may be evaluated by comparing the number of boating accidents in the area this year with the number last year. Likewise, a community organization may assess the impact of a block-watch program by comparing the number of crimes reported in the program area with the number reported in other areas in the community. Parkum (1985) evaluated the impact of a hospital volunteer program by measuring patient perceptions of the helpfulness of the volunteers.

According to Curtis and Fisher (1989), an organization that involves volunteers in a communitywide effort may develop standards that reflect the impact on the community as a whole. For example, a group of local television stations planned to assess the success of a teen pregnancy-prevention campaign it sponsored by measuring the impact of the program on the entire community. The program was to be judged successful if the city experienced at least a 10 percent decrease in the teen pregnancy rate.

Because impact evaluation looks at the consequences of a volunteer program in the broadest and most inclusive form, it is also the most challenging method of evaluation to conduct. The total impact of a large program is usually difficult to describe completely, and the benefits may be equally formidable to measure because of their extensive or their intangible nature. It is also difficult to ascertain the degree to which change occurs as a result of the program and the degree to which it occurs as a result of other factors. Some programs result in unanticipated impacts; others affect unintended populations. However, when large groups of people benefit from programs such as a pregnancy-prevention campaign, publicly available data that track demographic or economic changes may assist in quantifying the program's outcomes. No evaluation is complete if it does not assess the benefits provided to the larger population and demonstrate the broad consequences of a program.

The following illustration demonstrates how process, results, and impact measures are derived from program goals and objectives for a volunteer program serving central-city families.

> *Program Goal:* To increase the parenting skills of Spanish-speaking families by involving them in family-life education and support programs.
>
> *Objectives:* (1) to recruit ten bilingual-bicultural Hispanic volunteers, (2) to train ten Hispanic volunteers in the Nurturing model of family-life education, and (3) to involve twenty-five Spanish-speaking families in the family-life education and support programs.
>
> *Process Measures:* (1) Hours required by paid staff to prepare and conduct the recruitment drive and training sessions, (2) hours devoted by volunteers to training, (3) hours of involvement by other personnel from the agency, (4) number of volunteers recruited, (5) number of volunteers who complete training, (6) hours of service provided by volunteers, and (7) program costs.
>
> *Results Measures:* (1) Number of Spanish-speaking families served by the volunteers and (2) increase in client families' parenting skills as measured by a decrease in the number of incidents of abuse.
>
> *Impact Measures:* (1) Increase in service to persons from a population identified as hard to reach and (2) decrease in number of child-abuse and neglect incidents among the Spanish-speaking population as a whole.

How to Plan an Evaluation

Planning for an examination of the processes, results, and impacts of a program best occurs at the time the program is planned and before implementation begins. In other words, the evaluation plan should be an integral part of the overall program plan.

The evaluation plan describes each step of the process in detail and assigns responsibility for its performance. A clear scheme includes identification of the users and purposes of the evaluation, a statement of the program goals and objectives on which the evaluation will be based, a schedule of tasks and activities to be performed, specification of data to be gathered, and identification of the person or persons responsible.

Identifying Users and Purposes

Patton (1986), in emphasizing that evaluations should be developed with and designed for their users, presents an evaluation plan constructed to ensure that findings are useful to those with a vested interest in a program. His plan includes the following steps: (1) Identify the primary intended users of the evaluation, such as administrators, funders, clients, and volunteers. (2) Discuss with intended users the purpose and function of the evaluation and gain agreement on the relevant questions to be asked. (3) Work with intended users in making measurement and methods decisions so that they understand the strengths and weaknesses of the design and find the conclusions credible. (4) Engage intended users in interpreting findings, making judgments based on the data, and generating recommendations.

Whether one follows Patton's steps or not, certain advantages accrue from beginning the planning process with a clear identification of an evaluation's users and purposes. Such an approach distinguishes well-planned evaluations from "fishing expeditions" conducted to discover whatever may be found. Evaluations that lack clearly identified audiences and purposes are destined to be filed without being read. Evaluations designed with and for the user are likely to focus on specific needs, which minimizes the temptation to assess all aspects of a program and helps to guarantee that evaluation resources will be used in a cost-effective manner.

Stating Goals and Objectives

Key to the implementation of a successful evaluation is a statement of program goals and objectives, which should be unequivocal, measurable, and not in conflict with each other. Program goals state the anticipated impact of the program, and objectives describe the results in measurable terms.

Program evaluation is frequently impeded because goals and objectives are not clearly stated. The use of nonmeasurable objectives or ambiguously stated goals makes the direction of a program susceptible to misunderstanding; as a result, program planners, program leaders, and program evaluators may perceive the purpose of a program quite differently.

In addition to being impeded by ambiguity in the statement of goals and objectives, evaluations may suffer when goals lack consistency or are in conflict. For example, Utterback and Heyman (1984) report that a mental health center required its clinical staff to use 50 percent of their available time for direct service. This goal placed them in competition for clients with direct-service volunteers, hampering efforts to achieve another goal—the improvement of paid-staff/volunteer relations.

Scheduling Tasks and Activities

Three factors govern the scheduling of evaluation tasks and activities: the date the evaluation report is expected to be available, the date the program data will be available, and the number and complexity of tasks to be performed. The schedule should provide for the completion of preparatory events, such as organizing and training paid-staff and volunteers for their roles in the evaluation and preparing data-gathering instruments, prior to the availability of data. Gathering and analyzing data, developing conclusions, and framing recommendations should be sequenced between the two key dates.

Scheduling evaluation activities to fit within program milestones enhances the articulation between the program and the evaluation. Furthermore, the development of a timetable enables evaluators to perform their work in a timely fashion.

Specifying Required Data

Early identification of data to be collected as part of the evaluation plan makes the data-gathering process cost-effective and establishes the evaluation parameters, thereby reducing the concern and stress sometimes associated with program evaluation. A later section on how to gather data outlines the kinds of data needed.

Identifying Those Who Will Oversee and Conduct the Evaluation

Identification of the person or group responsible for the evaluation is an important element in the plan. Responsibility for program evaluation is most often assigned either to the administrator of volunteer programs or to another administrator whose responsibility includes planning and evaluation. The volunteer administrator is usually well-acquainted with any program involving volunteers and is in a position to develop an evaluation plan based on objective data to form the basis for a credible evaluation. Furthermore, an administrator of volunteer programs is usually responsible for making the modifications identified in the monitoring phase of program evaluation. Although responsibility for a program, as well as its evaluation, may challenge a volunteer administrator to be attentive to both responsibilities, effective program administrators understand evaluation to be an integral part of program development, whether specifically assigned or not.

Administrators with responsibility for funding, planning, or evaluation are able to frame an evaluation within an organization's mission and resource base. These administrators have the advantage of objectivity arising from lack of direct involvement with a program and at the same time are able to assess its effectiveness alongside other programs offered by an organization.

A group that may assume particular responsibilities in a program evaluation is the program advisory committee. Such a committee consists of knowledgeable and interested volunteers, staff, and clients chosen to provide oversight and expertise for a particular program. They perform this job by consulting with a program's administrators and staff.

In many instances, an advisory committee is charged with the oversight of an evaluation as well as with the responsibility for its timely completion. Advisory committees are particularly well-positioned to conduct the program monitoring required in formative evaluations (see the following discussion of formative evaluation); they may also be involved in the discussion of evaluation findings and the implementation of recommendations. Another important function of an advisory committee in evaluations is as a source of information because of members' knowledge of needs, goals, outcomes, and resource utilization. Miller (1987) advocates the active participation of an advisory committee in creating the evaluation design and assisting with gathering the data. Such involvement, says Miller, is possible because of the committee's distance from the program itself, and its participation in evaluation strengthens its advisory role.

Consultants, professional program evaluators, and program experts from outside the organization are sometimes enlisted to conduct the evaluation of a volunteer program. It is assumed that these persons bring to a program sufficient time and expertise to conduct an evaluation and sufficient freedom from organizational obligations to be objective. These assumptions should be confirmed before outside evaluators are hired.

The disadvantages of using outside evaluators is that the organizations may have limited involvement in the process and consequently limited ownership of the findings and recommendations. When persons from outside an organization are employed to conduct a program evaluation, they should consult with all those who will use the evaluation to determine the purpose and shape of the evaluation process, and they should involve both paid staff and volunteers in the process to the greatest extent possible. In addition, they should assure that procedures are in place for analyzing conclusions and implementing recommendations before their work is completed.

When to Evaluate

Most programs are evaluated both while they are being conducted and after they have been concluded. Processes that monitor the use of resources and the completion of tasks according to schedule are known as *formative evaluation*. Assessing the achievement of a program's goals at its completion is *summative evaluation*. Carefully designed evaluations will include both.

Formative Evaluation

Formative evaluation occurs throughout the course of program implementation. Its principal purpose is to monitor the program process by ascertaining that the program is being carried out according to the plan and by suggesting modifications or refinements that will improve chances that goals and objectives will be achieved. Formative evaluation monitors all aspects of a program's process, particularly the adequacy of resources assigned (both personnel and budgetary), the timing of activities, and the incremental achievement of objectives. Formative evaluation answers questions such as these: Is the project on schedule? Are the resources being expended and the objectives being achieved commensurate with projections? Is the implementation of the program consistent with the mission of the organization, given the time and resources being consumed?

Formative evaluation is usually conducted by the person responsible for the management of a program, someone who is in a position to make changes to assure successful accomplishment of a program's goals. Evaluation that is simultaneous with the program allows for data gathering from clients and participants, immediate feedback to service providers and participants, and concurrent planning for future programs.

In the following illustration, a program was modified on the basis of the findings from a formative evaluation:

> The communications committee of a volunteer center began a citywide recruitment drive for older adult volunteers. The drive was scheduled to last three months. As part of the initial phone interview, newly recruited volunteers were asked how they learned about the opportunity to volunteer. After the first three weeks, it became obvious that the vast majority (85 percent) of the new recruits came in response to three of the ten different methods being used to attract potential volunteers. Based on this formative evaluation, the committee decided to concentrate the recruitment efforts by increasing the amount of time, energy, and money spent on the three most productive methods.

Summative Evaluation

The purpose of summative evaluation is to ascertain the degree to which project goals and objectives have been achieved. For this reason, summative evaluation usually occurs at the conclusion of a project or program, when a complete summary statement can be made. Although results and outcomes are its chief focus, a summative evaluation also describes the resources and the process used by a particular program.

The principal users of a summative evaluation may be any of a program's stakeholders: funders, administrators, board members, volunteers, and clients may want to learn whether a particular program achieved its purpose, was cost-effective in its operation, and has promise of continuation.

Consider the following example:

A national funder of community-service programs requires year-end summative reports. Volunteer administrators are expected to provide information regarding the service-delivery process, including quantitative measures such as hours of service and number of clients. Measures of the extent to which program objectives were met are another integral component. Demographic characteristics of clients, such as age, gender, income, zip code, and race are required. Volunteer administrators also have the option of sharing program-related anecdotal information such as paid-staff and volunteer observations and client feedback. Finally, the funder requests a unit-of-service designation (number of hours or number of clients), which, when divided by total program costs, provides a cost per unit.

How to Gather Data

Most of the information used in program evaluation can be quantified by reducing it to numbers: the number of hours volunteered, the number of clients served, the number of dollars spent or saved.

However, some aspects of a volunteer program are not easily quantified. These aspects include the intangible benefits an organization enjoys, such as increased staff morale, improved community relations, increased interest in programs, reduced stress for staff, and increased loyalty to the organization or cause; they also include program outcomes, such as increased client satisfaction, improved well-being of clients or of everyone in a neighborhood, and increased support for a program in the community. Measuring these aspects of a volunteer program requires qualitative data. A good evaluation uses both quantitative and qualitative data in order to present a complete picture of a program.

Qualitative Data

Qualitative data are contained in narrative accounts: interviews, observations, organizational records. These data are then grouped according to subject matter and are used to describe those program outcomes that are not easily quantifiable.

Qualitative measures are used in the evaluation of volunteer programs for two principal reasons. First, many program benefits are difficult to quantify or are not quantifiable. Birnbaum (1991, p. 7) notes that a problem in evaluating educational programs is that education is a process of "converting tangible resources into intangible resources." (His statement is equally true of public-service programs.) And, as he points out, there is no broad consensus on what those intangibles are or ought to be, or on how to assess them. As a result, in many instances they are estimated and compared with budgetary costs. Such calculations are not necessarily wrong, according to Birnbaum, but they are incomplete.

The second reason to use qualitative measures, therefore, is to capture the uniqueness of a program involving volunteers. Karn (1982-1983, p. 2) argues that "dollars and cents will never capture the total contribution of a Big Brother or Big Sister, a rape crisis volunteer, a daily telephone reassurance call, a lobbyist or advocate at the State Legislature."

Curtis and Fisher (1989) describe three steps in the use of qualitative measures. The first is establishing outcome standards and measures of success in relation to program goals. One example of a qualitative outcome standard is "90 percent of program participants will report and describe increased ability to deal effectively with their anger and/or stress."

The second step is the collection of qualitative data to ascertain the degree to which the standards are met. These data may be collected through observations, interviews, or surveys, using a structured format to ensure that similar data are gathered from each respondent. Miller (1987) suggests that records of meetings, informal discussions with program administrators and staff members, and formal interviews with other program stakeholders may be useful. Client interviews and surveys use data from paid staff, clients, and volunteers to describe the nature of the relationship between volunteers and clients and particularly changes in the level of client development as the result of the program. Capturing such data in a qualitative format conveys much more of the spirit of a program than the numerical reporting that "x clients achieved their goals" or that "y visits were made by z volunteers."

Another way to gather qualitative data is through the use of goal-attainment scaling, a systematic way for paid staff, volunteers, and clients to assess the degree to which preestablished outcomes have been attained. Goal-attainment scaling assumes that for a given goal several outcomes are possible: the most favorable outcome, an outcome that is better than expected, the expected outcome, an outcome that is worse than expected, and the least favorable outcome. At the beginning of a program, each of these possible outcomes is specified: for example, the most favorable outcome for a teenage mother involved in a parenting program may be "an increase in behaviors that demonstrate nurturing and protective parenting" and the least favorable outcome may be "an increase in behaviors that are physically abusive to her children" or "withdrawing from the program." Program activities are assessed by locating outcomes on the goal-attainment scale: for example, six clients in the parenting program are achieving the most favorable outcome, and four clients are achieving the expected outcome. Goal-attainment scaling may be used to measure progress (as in formative evaluation) or to describe outcomes (as in summative evaluation).

Quantitative Data

Curtis and Fisher's (1989) third step is to integrate quantitative and qualitative data to present a complete picture of a program. A great amount of quantitative data is available through the records kept regularly by an organization. Some of these records describe the volunteer effort: the number of clients served, the length and extent of service provided to each, the number of volunteers providing service, the number of hours provided by each, the amount of training received by each, the rate of turnover of volunteers.

Other records describe the efforts of paid staff who work in conjunction with volunteers: the amount of staff time spent on particular activities such as screening, training, placing, supervising, and evaluating volunteers; the rate of paid-staff turnover; the amount of time spent training paid staff in volunteer supervision and relationships; the amount of time the administrator of volunteer programs spends in recruitment, coordination, supervision, and training directly related to the volunteer program; the amount of time the administrator of volunteer programs spends in the performance of non–volunteer-related responsibilities.

In addition, the program budget can be checked to determine the total amount of monetary resources used. These resources generally include staff costs, such as the salaries, fringe benefits, and expense allowances of the administrator of volunteer programs, and of other staff who have direct responsibility for various components of the volunteer program. Monetary resources also include program costs, such as the cost of staff time for training, the cost of training and other program materials, and advertising and recruitment costs. To both staff and program costs is added the cost of the organization's administration and overhead.

Because most organizations use line-item budgets—that is, budgets in which the annual cost of a staff person or of a program component is contained in a "line"—care must be exercised to include only that portion of a line item that relates to the volunteer program. For example, the amount of time the executive director spends training volunteers should be prorated and included as the cost of the volunteer program, but the amount of time the administrator of volunteer programs spends representing the entire agency

in the community or administering non-volunteer-related programs should be prorated and subtracted from the total cost of the
volunteer program.

Quantitative data may also be gathered from other sources.
Miller (1987) suggests using questionnaires and interviews to tap
the insights and opinions of selected groups and individuals who
are served by a program, such as clients, or who are in a position
to influence a program or to be influenced by it. Utterback and
Heyman (1984) recommend the use of peer reviews, where staff
members rate the performance of their volunteer counterparts in
order to compare actual procedures against standards. Such surveys,
questionnaires, and review forms may be constructed in such a way
that the data are easily quantified.

Program evaluations may include data that describe staff
reaction, volunteer reaction, and client reaction to a project. Allen
(1987) points out that because many volunteer/client interactions
take place away from the agency, staff have limited opportunity to
observe them directly. Information about those interactions can be
obtained by requiring volunteers in decentralized programs to
maintain records detailing the length, frequency, and nature of
their meetings with clients or by assigning a staff member familiar
with the client population and the program to meet regularly with
the volunteer and the client.

How to Analyze Data

The analysis of data in evaluations of volunteer programs consists
mainly of assigning value and comparing benefits to costs.

Assignment of Value

The first step is the quantification of the information secured. An
important part of this step is the assignment of monetary value to
various data, particularly data on the time contributed by paid staff
and volunteers. Paid-staff costs are usually calculated by adding
together a staff member's salary and the cost of his or her fringe
benefits to arrive at a figure for annual compensation; this figure
is multiplied by the percentage of work time the staff member has

been involved, either officially or unofficially, with the volunteer program. In a study, Baker and Murawski (1986) estimated paid-staff cost per hour by dividing the median annual gross salary of paid staff plus the cost of employee benefits by the number of working hours.

The conversion of volunteer time to dollars allows for a useful comparison between the cost of paid-staff involvement and the value of volunteer involvement in a particular program and is therefore widely advocated. However, there is much less unanimity on how to calculate the value of the time contributed by volunteers. Some analysts multiply the total number of hours provided by volunteers by the federal minimum wage. Others multiply the total number of hours of volunteer service by the average hourly wage for nonprofessionals within the organization (Utterback and Heyman, 1984).

The costs of volunteer programs are calculated by dividing the total expenses for the volunteer program by the number of hours of volunteer service provided, yielding a cost per hour of volunteer service. This figure can then be compared with similar costs in other programs, with the cost of using paid staff, or with the federal minimum wage.

The use of the federal minimum wage, the national median wage, or average hourly wage estimates in these calculations tends to put a low value on volunteer services and gives credence to the assumption that volunteers provide little more than free unskilled labor. To redress this undervaluation, Karn (1982–1983, p. 3) developed a means for assessing the value of volunteer efforts by assigning replacement costs at "fair market value or purchase price of parallel paid services"—in other words, by assigning the costs that would be incurred if the services were purchased from paid employees rather than provided by volunteers. In order to determine replacement costs, the program evaluator identifies a paid employment classification in which the duties are judged to be equivalent to those of a volunteer. The annual salary for someone so classified is added to the value of that person's fringe benefits to determine the total value of usual compensation. Hours paid for but not worked (holidays, vacations, leave) are subtracted from the annual work hours to determine the actual number of hours worked annually. Total annual compensation is divided by the actual numbers of hours worked annually to establish the dollar value of each hour of volunteer time.

Karn notes that the challenge of this method is to find paid classifications in which responsibilities closely parallel a volunteer's responsibilities. He illustrates with these "equivalents": for a board member, the equivalent is a figure 10 to 20 percent greater than the salary of the executive director of an organization; for a Little League coach, equivalent value is the salary of a playground supervisor; for a Big Brother or Big Sister, the equivalent value is the salary of an outreach worker. Another problem, according to Karn, is that many volunteers underreport their hours by counting only the time they are engaged in direct service.

Comparisons of Benefits and Costs

The relationships between various aspects of a volunteer program are often key pieces of information in evaluations; these relationships are expressed as ratios and are used in general to compare the costs of a volunteer program with the estimated value of the service provided. Such ratios are popular with program administrators for two reasons: most of the data are routinely collected and readily available within an organization, and funders and administrators can easily use such ratios to compare requests for support. The following are ratios frequently employed in the evaluation of volunteer programs.

Turnover Ratio. This ratio compares the portion of volunteers retained (rate of turnover) with the hours spent on volunteer administration (or on particular activities such as screening, training, placement, evaluation) (Gamm and Kassab, 1983).

Cost per Hour of Volunteer Service. This ratio is derived by dividing the costs of the program by the number of volunteer hours (Sues and Wilson, 1987). This figure can be compared with similar figures from other volunteer programs or other organizations and with the minimum wage or the average wage in the sponsoring organization.

Cost per Unit of Volunteer Service. Caraway and Van Gilder (1985) divided the costs (staff salaries, equipment, printing, postage, and telephones) to maintain a program that screened and referred persons suffering from hypertension by the number of screenings at a given site, thereby establishing an efficiency ratio. By using this ratio they could compare the efficiency (cost per screening) of one site with others and of programs involving volunteers with programs involving paid professionals.

Clients Satisfied/Clients Served. This measure of effectiveness compares the number of clients satisfied with the service of volunteers with the total number of clients served (Gamm and Kassab, 1983).

Cost/Value of Volunteer Program. This frequently used measure of efficiency divides the dollar value of volunteer services by the dollar costs of volunteer services to an organization. A variation of this ratio is the assessment of net benefits derived by subtracting the costs of a volunteer program from the dollar value of volunteer services. In variations described by Gamm and Kassab (1983), the evaluator calculates the number of clients served by volunteers per hour, the number of hours of volunteer service per hour of volunteer administration, or the estimated dollar value of volunteer service divided by the actual expenditures for volunteer services.

Costs/Benefits. Many ratios are described as cost/benefit. However, most can more accurately be entitled cost/value of volunteer services because they compare the cost with the estimated value of the work of volunteers in an organization. A cost/benefit analysis compares the cost of a volunteer program with the value of the changes it brings in the lives of clients or with the value of the program results to clients. A volunteer literacy-tutoring program would calculate its benefits by estimating the dollar value of learning to read for its clients and their families. A docent program in a museum would estimate the value of the benefits of its service by calculating the dollar value of having citizens learn about the museum exhibits.

According to Peterson (1986, p. 30), "The purpose of [benefit/cost analysis] is generally to determine if program objectives are economically feasible. After evaluating the benefits and costs of alternatives for dealing with a problem, three questions are answered via [this] procedure: (1) are benefits greater than costs; . . . (2) among alternative courses of action, which has the most attractive benefit-cost ratio; . . . and (3) what is the net benefit of costs produced by this alternative?"

Cost/benefit ratios are often difficult to calculate for volunteer services because benefits cannot be measured in dollars. As Karn affirms (1982–1983, p. 10), "This is equally true of social service, cultural, educational, or recreation programs because market prices are not available to appraise their social contributions. . . . A true cost-benefit analysis of a volunteer juvenile-offender program would measure the dollar cost of supporting the volunteers versus the dollar value of the changed behavior of the clients resulting from the volunteer activity. This is a virtual impossibility."

How to Interpret Results

Accuracy and Believability

Concern for the accuracy and believability of findings drawn from evaluations compels mention of two concepts used by researchers and evaluators: validity, which indicates that particular data do in fact measure what they purport to measure, and reliability, which indicates that a particular instrument or data-gathering technique will obtain consistent results over time. Posavac and Carey (1989) suggest that measures that focus on objective information and behavior will likely be more valid and more reliable than those that are undefined or vague. They also suggest that believability is enhanced when staff members contribute to the development of evaluation design and measures.

Utterback and Heyman (1984, p. 229) report that evaluations of volunteer programs are often "replete with impressionistic, unverified data and conclusions, which, in the absence of control groups or base rates, must be interpreted with caution." Although it often is not possible to have control groups and other research components that are necessary for drawing verifiable inferences, the accuracy and believability of findings are enhanced when evaluations use multiple measures to confirm and verify one another. For example, a program evaluation might assess client satisfaction using a survey that probes behavioral change, interviews with clients, and objective data that describe client behavior. Patton asserts (1991, p. 10) that "programs that make a real difference . . . yield multiple indicators of impact—both quantitative and qualitative."

The Politics of Evaluation

Anyone who has evaluated a program or participated in a program undergoing evaluation has learned firsthand that neutral evaluation is impossible. Because an evaluation influences a program's continuation and character, those associated with it as leaders, participants, clients, and other stakeholders find themselves to be affected, either directly or indirectly, by the findings and conclusions. Sensitivity to evaluation findings is heightened when program evaluators fail to involve program participants in planning and implementing the evaluaticn or fail to provide adequate information about the evaluation's purpose and process.

Responses to evaluation range from ownership to resistance. By involving as many stakeholders as possible in the evaluation process, evaluators increase the potential for program ownership to be broadened and for evaluation outcomes to be taken seriously. When various stakeholders are able to contribute to and participate in the planning and evaluation of a program, they are likely to facilitate the process, have confidence in the findings, and implement the recommendations.

Stakeholders and other interested parties who are excluded from the process are likely to respond in nonproductive ways ranging from resistance to hostility. Resistance occurs when program participants are unclear about how the findings will benefit them or the program or are suspicious that the findings may cast the program in a negative light; resistant behavior ranges from lack of enthusiasm to lack of cooperation. Hostility occurs when stakeholders believe that the findings will be so negative that their jobs or the program or both will be endangered; they focus their energy on denying access to important data, criticizing the process, and discrediting the findings.

One popular way of enhancing the credibility of evaluation

findings is to establish a special committee of volunteers, paid staff, and administrators to provide advice on and oversight of the evaluation process. Whether or not the evaluators are from outside the organization, an advisory committee representative of various stakeholder groups often provides an important bridge between those conducting the evaluation and those responsible for implementing its findings.

How to Present Evaluation Findings

A comprehensive written report of a program evaluation includes a statement of the purpose and objectives of the evaluation, a discussion of the design, and a description of the data-gathering process and data analysis. Information on how, by whom, and when particular activities in the evaluation plan were performed is also included. The report presents the results of all the measures employed and of the data analysis. When the data are quantitative, findings are presented in tables and figures combined with an explanatory narrative. When the data are qualitative, findings are presented in a narrative that incorporates quotations and descriptions of observations as illustrations.

Following the presentation of the results of the evaluation, the evaluator usually interprets the findings and draws conclusions on the basis of the data presented. The conclusion section summarizes the findings as they relate to the purpose and objectives of the evaluation and draws inferences about the program's effectiveness and efficiency on the basis of these findings. Finally, a series of recommendations is provided for revising the program and developing future programs.

Role of the Volunteer Administrator

Administrators of volunteer programs may assume any of a number of roles in a program evaluation. Often they are required to plan and organize the evaluation, to implement it, or to interpret the findings in order to justify or improve the program for which they are responsible. In other situations, administrators of volunteer programs are expected to cooperate with an evaluator who has been selected from outside the organization and then to implement the recommendations the outside evaluator presents. In either case, volunteer administrators are well served by possessing the knowledge and skills required in program evaluation so that their decision making and recordkeeping can be guided by the continuing need to demonstrate program efficiency and effectiveness. Furthermore, volunteer administrators should be incorporating evaluation designs into their program plans and should be gathering the appropriate data as the programs continue so that as managers they are able to assess the continuing effectiveness of their programs.

Conclusion

Organizations that involve volunteers in their programs are the stewards of invaluable human resources. The unpaid nature of volunteer service notwithstanding, such organizations are frequently requested to demonstrate that the use of volunteers is an efficient way to provide services and that a particular volunteer program contributes toward the achievement of an organization's mission. Furthermore, program leaders are continually being challenged to upgrade the quality of service and to discover ways to improve their programs. The outcome of a program evaluation may influence the decision to continue a program, to fund a program, or to improve a program in particular ways. Those in leadership roles are in key positions to increase a volunteer program's support and quality as the result of their knowledge and use of effective program-evaluation strategies.

9

Professionalism
in Volunteer Administration

We have concerned ourselves until now with the various responsibilities and functions associated with the role of volunteer administrator. In this chapter, we focus on the larger professional context in which volunteer administrators operate and on the steps administrators of volunteer programs have taken toward professionalization. We also discuss philosophical and ethical issues germane to volunteer administration.

Movement Toward Professionalization

Although professions date from the early Middle Ages, the advent of many new occupations and the desire of their practitioners to be regarded as professionals have led to an interest in classifying the professions. Numerous lists of arbitrary criteria describe bona fide professions and distinguish them from other vocations and occupations. Although workers in most occupations want to be regarded as professionals, according to Wilensky (1964), out of thousands of identifiable occupations, only thirty or forty have been fully professionalized.

Houle (1980) differentiates absolute and dynamic criteria for professions: absolute criteria are used as fixed canons to classify some occupations as professions, and dynamic criteria are used as specific goals toward which an occupation can strive in its professionalizing efforts. Using this approach, Houle shifts the focus from verifying particular occupations as professions to engaging in a professionalizing process that guides occupations and vocations as they develop the characteristics of a profession. The degree of professionalization of an occupation may be assessed on the basis of fourteen dynamic characteristics intrinsic to the professionalizing process. The first five characteristics describe practitioners of a professionalizing vocation. They should:

1. Be concerned with clarifying the profession's "defining function or functions" (p. 35) and with articulating the unifying concepts that constitute its mission.
2. Master the essential information and theory that constitute its knowledge base and be knowledgeable about the theoretical disciplines that contribute to that base.
3. Be able to use theoretical bodies of knowledge to solve problems that arise in practice or in the practical affairs of people.
4. Have available and use a substantial body of knowledge and technique that has grown out of the vocation's practical applications.
5. Enhance themselves through the serious study of topics not directly related to their occupation.

The remaining nine characteristics describe the vocation as a whole. It should:

6. Establish formal procedures to transmit its essential body of knowledge and technique to all recognized practitioners before they enter service and throughout their careers.
7. Use formal means to test the capacity of individual practitioners to perform their duties at an acceptable level and when appropriate to license those qualified to do so.
8. Create for its members a subculture with distinctive attributes.
9. Use legal support and formal administrative rulings to protect the special rights and privileges of practitioners.
10. Encourage the general public to be aware of the high quality of the work done by practitioners of the vocation.
11. Establish a tradition or formal code of ethical practice that is refined in the light of changing circumstances.

12. Establish and enforce standards of practice that result in penalties for those who are incompetent or fail to uphold ethical standards.
13. Establish and maintain clear relationships with allied occupations.
14. Define the relationship between practitioners and those who use their services.

To summarize, a vocation in the process of professionalizing would be engaged in developing a knowledge base, setting standards for entry into practice, setting standards for acceptable practice, creating a distinctive subculture for its members, and presenting itself to the public. To the degree that the vocation of volunteer administration is seeking to achieve these goals, it is engaged in professionalization. The following sections discuss these aspects of the professionalizing process of volunteer administration in the light of current research and activity.

Knowledge Base

The field of volunteer administration is engaged in a process to describe its own knowledge base. Although the interaction between a manager and unpaid staff persons may be unique, the literature describing it relies heavily on what is known in the fields of business management, personnel management, and public-service administration. In fact, considerable effort, illustrated by Cronk's study (1982), has been invested to show that managers of volunteer programs have responsibilities similar to those of other managers. Ellis and Noyes (1990) describe the strongly contextual underpinnings of the evolution of the role of volunteer administrator. They point out how information about volunteering itself is often contextual—how volunteering is described mainly in terms of the setting in which the volunteer works—making it doubly difficult to segregate a knowledge base unique to volunteerism and volunteer administration.

In their national survey of the administration of volunteer programs, Stubblefield and Miles (1986, p. 7) found that 57 percent of the respondents regarded volunteer administration as their primary vocational orientation, 30 percent preferred employment in other fields, 40 percent had greater loyalty to the employing institution than to volunteer administration, and 33 percent regarded their current position as an intermediate point in their administrative career at their employing institution. In describing how they achieved their present positions, 34 percent said the position evolved from previous employment, 26 percent pursued the position, 20 percent said the position evolved from previous volunteer work, and 18 percent came to the position "by happenstance." Combining responses to these two questions leaves one with the picture of a field where the institutional context seems to overshadow the practice of the vocation.

Given that approximately one-third of the practitioners expect to advance in careers other than volunteer administration, a knowledge base linked with those of other management vocations and supporting readily transferable skills would seem to serve this population best. One might anticipate therefore that the development of a discrete knowledge base will progress only as volunteer administration develops a strong professional identity and a clearly identifiable career ladder and as volunteer administrators increase their commitment to volunteer administration as a life's work.

Standards for Entry

Stubblefield and Miles's (1986) survey revealed great diversity in how volunteer administrators are prepared for their positions plus an absence of any general societal recognition that volunteer administration involves specialized knowledge and requires intensive training. Approximately 33 percent of the practitioners responding had less than a baccalaureate degree, 39 percent had a baccalaureate degree, and 28 percent had a master's degree; areas of study varied greatly, but only 1 percent received degrees in volunteer administration.

These data and practice indicate that standards and prerequisites for entry are most generally established by organizations who hire volunteer administrators. In contrast, prerequisites for persons with responsibility and expertise in other areas, such as social work, teaching, the ministry, and fire-fighting administration, are set by their profession. At present, little evidence suggests that standards for entrance into the field of volunteer administration will be broadly accepted or universally applied.

Standards for Practice

The establishment of a performance-based assessment program for the certification of volunteer administrators by the AVA is a significant step in the professionalization process. This program, developed in the early 1980s from research by Rehnborg (1982), consists of competency-based standards in four functional areas (program planning and organization; staffing and directing; controlling; and agency, community, and professional relations) that have been recognized by the AVA as constituting the practice of volunteer administration. Practitioners may describe their work in these areas and present examples of it to demonstrate acceptable levels of professional practice. Stubblefield and Miles (1986) learned that 15 percent of their respondents had completed and another 15 percent were working toward certification. Resource B contains details on AVA's certification standards.

In addition to being a pioneering effort to set standards of acceptable practice for the field, the AVA certification program presents an opportunity for practitioners to demonstrate their competence apart from the level of their education or the depth of their commitment to the field. In this way, the AVA is able to promote standards for practice without having to address difficult issues related to entry standards, career progression, or public acceptance of the certification standards.

Distinctive Subculture

Significant progress toward professionalization has been made through the creation of formal associations such as the AVA, an international organization for persons in this field of practice; national organizations for volunteer administrators who work in particular environments, such as the American Association for Museum Volunteers; and local formal networks of volunteer administrators. Most of these organizations have as their purposes socializing new members, improving practice through continuing professional education, encouraging members to maintain certain levels of competence, and providing personal support. Some also serve as clearinghouses for information about open positions.

National organizations have published or encouraged publication of journals that serve the field through the presentation of current theory, research, and practice: *The Journal of Volunteer Administration, Voluntary Action Leadership,* and the *Nonprofit and Voluntary Sector Quarterly* (formerly the *Journal of Voluntary Action Research*). By setting standards for practice, disseminating information about the field, and encouraging the development of relevant literature, the AVA has been instrumental in developing the knowledge base of volunteer administration.

Awareness

The public is apprised of activities in this field of practice by local, national, and international organizations. Independent Sector has enriched the volunteer enterprise by its advocacy and research; organizations such as the American Red Cross have conducted and distributed studies on volunteerism and the management of volunteer efforts. Local organizations of volunteer administrators and volunteer centers also promote a general awareness of the role of volunteering in our society and the contribution of the volunteer administrator.

Issues of Professionalization

A discussion of the professionalization of volunteer administration often focuses on two major points: the feasibility of professionalization and the advisability of professionalization. Arguments related to feasibility usually focus on the broad diversity of the field as it is presently constructed: the vocation is practiced in many different settings by paid and unpaid, full- and part-time volunteer administrators whose educational background ranges from having a high school diploma to having a doctorate and whose job-related experience ranges from being a volunteer to being a middle- or upper-level manager. Broad differences in responsibility result from this diversity, as does degree of identification with the profession. For some volunteer administrators, that title describes their main responsibility; others have different titles from which their principal identity comes (pastor, for example), although the responsibility for volunteer administration is nevertheless contained in their job descriptions.

Discussions of the feasibility of professionalization usually center on how to unify so diverse a practice rather than on how to eliminate such diversity. Discussants raise the negative specter of standardization and conformity but present positive notions of increased strength and impact resulting from increased cohesion in the description and practice of the profession.

Questions of the advisability of professionalization are more difficult to answer than questions about feasibility because agreement about benefits and costs is elusive. The quest for professionalization seems driven by strong forces, such as the need of volunteer administrators for professional respect and recognition as skilled program and personnel managers and the desire to enhance their competence and level of practice. Additional benefits to be gained from professionalization include improving service to clients, increasing the visibility of volunteerism, receiving increased public recognition for volunteer administrators' skills, gaining respect within the organizations where they are employed, and improving their fringe benefits and salaries.

Ilsley (1990) describes some of the dangers of professionalization: the creation of a distance between professional organizations and their members; the creation of a distance between volunteer administrators and volunteers; the imposition of bureaucratic rules and policies; an unnecessary increase in resources devoted to selection, training, certification, specialization, and supervision of volunteers; and an emphasis on standardization of services provided by volunteers. Ilsley concludes that "professionalism tends to produce an increased rigidity, an organizational 'hardening of the arteries,' that alienates volunteers. Rather than being simply welcomed as people who have a desire to serve, entering volunteers are screened, trained, supervised, and fitted into predetermined slots. They are treated like interchangeable objects rather than like people with individual interests and abilities" (p. 87).

The controversy over professionalization is doubtless more complex than these paragraphs indicate. The challenge to those who practice in the field of volunteer administration is to work toward professionalization without destroying the initiative and spontaneity of volunteers and the uniqueness of their contributions.

Philosophical and Ethical Issues

This section offers an overview of the philosophical and ethical foundations of volunteer administration. How does one link a personal philosophy to that of an organization and its volunteer program? What changes take place in individuals' values and philosophies when competing or different values and philosophies are part of the environment in which they function?

Philosophy of the Profession

Volunteer administrators establish their identity by defining a personal philosophy of volunteerism and by adopting a distinct set of standards and guidelines for ethical practice. The Association for Volunteer Administration (AVA) has played a leadership role by including philosophy of volunteerism as a major component of its performance-based certification program and by establishing a set of standards and ethics for the profession of volunteer administration. The AVA requires candidates for certification in volunteer administration to prepare a written statement describing their personal philosophy of volunteerism and their view of the role of the volunteer administrator. Its Certification Panel of Assessment looks for evidence of consistency between candidates' philosophy of volunteerism and their beliefs regarding the role of the professional volunteer administrator by examining how these are demonstrated in their practice. It also encourages the development of an organizational philosophy of volunteerism.

In 1975, the AVA adopted a philosophy that established the profession's role as facilitator and mobilizer of human resources. The leadership, activities, and structure provided by the volunteer administrator enable needs to be met; create a social climate that makes the fulfillment of needs possible; provide for the involvement of people in decision-making processes that affect them; contribute to creative and responsible social development and change; and enhance and extend the work of professional and other paid staff. The AVA's guiding principles are based on a commitment to social responsibility, an understanding of the need of every person to express concern for others, and the concepts of dignity and self-determinism. The AVA's "Professional Ethics in Volunteer Services Administration" is reproduced as Resource A.

Personal Philosophy

The capacity to contribute one's time and other personal resources to social causes and voluntary organizations is an enduring human quality that has become essential in democratic societies. Voluntary action has been a constant throughout history, and the motivations for it have changed little through time. These motivations include the following:

- Enlightened self-interest based on need and an understanding of the mutual dependence of individuals and groups
- A desire to preserve and enhance the values and social order of society
- A need to do the "right thing"
- Religious duty (such as "Christian charity")
- Altruism and the conviction that the meaning and purpose of life can be discovered by giving of oneself to others
- Self-improvement and self-healing
- Simple "neighborliness"
- A desire to show gratitude for one's own good fortune by giving to those less fortunate

According to O'Connell (1986), it is important that volunteer administrators and others who work to preserve and strengthen volunteerism understand and nurture all roots of voluntary activity and participation. The manner in which volunteer administrators do so, however, will be shaped by their personal philosophy of volunteerism and their beliefs regarding the role of volunteer administrator. The following excerpts from philosophy statements developed by individuals who have attained the AVA's professional credential, Certified in Volunteer Administration (C.V.A.), illustrate personal philosophies of volunteerism.

Skillingstad (1986) believes a major part of her role as volunteer administrator is to help "unleash the motivation within individuals to participate actively in society and work to make a difference." Similarly, Lawson (1986) believes that the professional in volunteer administration is in a position to positively influence volunteers by affirming their gifts of time and talent, thereby encouraging volunteer growth and development. She sees herself as a partner with volunteers in their search for the skills, insights, experiences, and gifts that "they need to identify and use in order to truly be themselves." She feels that volunteer administrators are "in the best position to link people with gifts of skill and time and love with those who need what they can give."

Mason (1986) defines volunteers as "people who freely choose to take an active role in addressing social problems and humanitarian issues that are not related to their source of livelihood." Whether their jobs are performed within a formal organization or as part of an informal effort, volunteers are distinguished by providing more than what is expected of all citizens or members of a group. Furthermore, Mason views volunteerism as nonsalaried employment that provides tangible compensation. Each individual's "pay" is unique: socialization and friendship; improved physical, mental, or spiritual health; increased self-knowledge; the acquisition of new and marketable skills; or a sense of belonging and contributing to the betterment of a community. Mason links his philosophy to his practice by ensuring that volunteers receive the type of payment they need.

Waldner (1986) and Curtis (1986) share the philosophy that personal experience as a volunteer is essential to effective performance as a volunteer administrator. According to Waldner, "Perhaps this is the bottom line: one has to believe in volunteerism and be a volunteer to fully appreciate the privilege of volunteer management." Curtis attributes her understanding and acceptance of a wide variety of volunteer motivations to her years of personal experience as a volunteer. Because her reasons for volunteering changed as she grew and entered new phases of life, she is able to accept others' diverse and changing reasons for volunteering and work with them to identify positions and responsibilities that satisfy their needs and interests.

The challenge to volunteer administrators is to integrate these personal philosophies of volunteerism within their programs in a way that is compatible with the missions and philosophies of their organizations and that will continue to be compatible even when the needs of the organization change. As is illustrated in the following example, volunteer administrators often must balance the changing, pressing needs of the organization and the contrasting needs of volunteers.

An organization consisting of four distinct volunteer programs, each headed by a different volunteer administrator, was having a difficult time attracting and retaining minority volunteers. When lack of minority involvement began to affect its ability to compete successfully for certain sources of funds, the executive director assigned the volunteer administrators the annual goal of increasing the number of minority volunteers in each of their programs by 20 percent. Their performance evaluations and merit raises would be based to a large degree on the extent to which this goal was met.

In the past, the organization had prided itself on the fact that its current volunteer staff received notice of new volunteer opportunities within the organization before the general public. The volunteer administrators had been in philosophical agreement that current volunteers should have the option to participate in a new way if it met their interests and needs, even if a program might lose a good volunteer as a result. However, the pressure to meet the 20 percent goal for minority involvement caused two of the volunteer administrators to behave in a manner inconsistent with that philosophy; they neglected to inform their current minority volunteer staff of opportunities for involvement outside of their programs.

The internal competition among programs in this case was diminishing the integrity of the organization's philosophy of volunteer involvement and making it difficult for the volunteer administrators to maintain their commitment to meeting the needs of all volunteers.

Organizational Philosophy

Some organizations have developed their own philosophies of volunteerism. The American Red Cross, for example, has articulated its beliefs in the following ten principles (Smith, 1989):

1. We can broaden our nation's volunteer force by removing barriers to volunteering.
2. Volunteers are not "free."
3. Volunteers contribute more than meets the eye.
4. "Volunteer" does not mean "amateur."
5. Volunteers and the organizations they serve must meet each other's expectations.
6. Volunteers must never be exploited.
7. Volunteers make excellent middle and senior managers.
8. When recruiting volunteers, it is more important to place the right person in the job than to attract volunteers at random.
9. We can help shape government policies on volunteerism.
10. Everyone benefits when nonprofit organizations collaborate.

These guiding organizational principles provide a firm philosophical foundation on which volunteer administrators and other staff can develop volunteer positions and recruit volunteers.

Ethical Foundations

An ethical code for each profession begins with an analysis of the function that profession has in society and identifies the restraints that will make the profession most effective. It sets forth the unique rules and guidelines governing the actions of members of that profession. Core ethical principles common to most professions are honesty, integrity, loyalty, fairness, concern for others, respect for others, performance of civic duty, pursuit of excellence, personal accountability and responsibility, and preservation of the public trust. A professional code of ethics sets forth the worthy objectives of the profession and, in detail, those standards of conduct that must be met if these objectives are to be achieved. A code of ethics for volunteer administration provides a set of useful, standardized expectations for behavior that allow both beginning and experienced administrators to clarify to themselves and others the moral foundations of their practice.

In addition to a philosophy of volunteerism, each volunteer administrator must also adopt a professional code of ethics. The moral education of beginning professionals starts during the course of their initiation and socialization into the profession. According to Pellegrino, Veatch, and Langan (1991, p. 142), "The moral life is essentially a reflection on practice, and we are drawn into such reflection as we learn from skilled practitioners." Volunteer administrators often learn habitual behaviors and traditions of conduct from observing the actions of their peers.

Michael Oakeshott (cited in Pellegrino, Veatch, and Langan, 1991, p. 140) suggests, however, that ethical behavior based simply on traditions of conduct that are learned from others tends to be unreflective and free of hesitation. Practitioners whose ethics are based solely on tradition may lack self-critical powers and be unable to distinguish their vision of virtue from "the way we do things." Oakeshott encourages another form of ethical behavior in which "activity is determined, not by habit, . . . but by the reflective application of [a] moral criterion." This approach requires critical self-reflection in order to defend one's morals. According to Oakeshott, education in the moral life cannot come primarily from observing and following the behaviors of others; instead, intellectual training in a system of principles and how to apply and defend them is needed. Individuals who adopt a formal professional code of ethics act self-consciously, aware of the grounds on which their actions rest and prepared to defend those grounds.

Professionals who follow this approach to ethics are not likely to act simply on the basis of "how we do things." They are too self-critical, and their decision-making process is too systematic for that. The pause for reflection that is always needed before action is taken can be paralyzing, however, undermining the ability to act habitually and confidently. A combination of the approaches described by Pellegrino and by Oakeshott provides a rich basis for ethical decision making and professional practice.

Ethical Concerns

Professional ethics in volunteer administration deals with questions that are at the center of many modern dilemmas and that have wide ramifications. For instance, if an organization delivers essential services to disabled persons by involving volunteers, is the organization enabling government to neglect its responsibility for providing those services to which disabled persons are entitled by law? Do voluntary organizations prevent the development of paying jobs by involving volunteers as staff and, in doing so, do they contribute to the problem of unemployment?

Ethical questions encountered in the management of volunteer efforts usually do not have clear answers. They rarely involve a simple choice between obvious good and obvious evil; answers may appear justifiable in one sense yet may be denounced as unethical from another viewpoint. It is nevertheless necessary to raise the questions, even when answers prove elusive, and to adopt a set of principles for use in thinking and making decisions about ethical issues. In doing so, volunteer administrators must consider their responsibility to the volunteer, clients, the organization, other staff (both paid and unpaid), and the public, to say nothing of their own immediate supervisors. Because of their special relationship with each of these groups, volunteer administrators have moral duties that are both complex and unique.

Ethics in volunteer administration is a wide-ranging topic that easily deserves to be the focus of an entire book. We offer here an introduction to ethical concerns in volunteer management by examining confidentiality, conflicts between professionals, and the definition of *volunteer*.

Confidentiality. An ethical concern shared by all volunteer administrators on a number of levels is confidentiality: of client information known by volunteers, of volunteer files and performance reviews, and of information about the personal lives of volunteer staff. Confidentiality rules prevent the disclosure to third parties of information acquired in the course of performing professional duties. These rules have their origins in the ordinary promise to keep in confidence information shared by friends.

Professional confidentiality does not require a promise not to divulge each time information is gained. Rather it rests on a tacit assumption that everything disclosed is to remain confidential. It is frequently bound by law, most notably in professions such as personnel, counseling, and medicine. A departure from confidentiality is difficult to justify morally. Reasons that may suffice for a breach of ordinary confidentiality between friends do not suffice in professional situations, where serving the public interest, protecting the divulger, and protecting others are distinguishing factors.

The following example illustrates the complexities that may arise in dealing with issues related to confidentiality.

A volunteer administrator had been told by an adult male volunteer that he had tested positive for the HIV virus. A few weeks later, a female volunteer told her that she had begun dating the male volunteer. The volunteer administrator felt the young woman should be aware of the man's health status. Rather than disclosing the privileged information, she spoke with the male volunteer, who promised to inform the young woman.

Both professional and personal relations in the volunteer setting require handling information with the utmost sensitivity in order to safeguard the confidentiality of volunteers, professionals, and clients.

Professional Conflicts. Volunteer administrators are often in the difficult position of working within two different professions: volunteer administration and another profession such as social work, health, education, culture, or the arts. What happens when the aims of the two different professions come into conflict? The challenge to each profession in this case is to be faithful to its own mission and ethics while at the same time recognizing that the other profession also has a rightful claim to its standards of conduct. Resolving these issues requires that a delicate balance be maintained and that communication within the organization be strong, as is illustrated by the following case:

> One of the goals of an urban museum of human history was to promote cross-cultural understanding through its educational exhibits. Volunteers had successfully completed a training program to prepare them to lead educational tours of the African exhibit hall for elementary school children. Several school chaperones contacted the volunteer administrator to report a volunteer whom they felt had presented negative, stereotypical images along with inaccuracies in content about African cultures during the tour. The volunteer administrator held a discussion about the matter with the volunteer, who agreed to reattend the training program. The curator of the African exhibit, however, felt the volunteer's lack of sensitivity to cultural issues would not be changed through a repeat of the training and insisted he be dismissed.

Here, the volunteer administrator's interest in facilitating the development of the volunteer conflicted with the interest of the curator, who was concerned for the integrity of the exhibit. In order to maintain positive relationships within an organization, volunteer administrators should recognize the professional interests of other staff and negotiate solutions to such interprofessional conflicts.

Definition of Volunteer. A topic of much debate among volunteer administrators, leaders of their organizations, and volunteers centers around the question, "Who is a volunteer?" The answer depends to a large degree on one's definition of volunteerism. For example, if volunteering is viewed simply as the performance of helping activities without monetary reimbursement, how do loaned executives, participants in Volunteers in Service to America, and other stipend volunteers, fit within this definition? What if volunteers are reimbursed for transportation, meals, and other expenses incurred? Does this reimbursement affect their status? The trend for judges to order community-service hours as "payment" for certain types of criminal offenses raises questions regarding the degree to which this form of helping can be considered voluntary. Also, how are these individuals to be integrated with an organization's regular volunteer staff? Similarly, high school and college students who participate in internship programs may or may not be considered volunteers. Do the requirements of an internship program and the fact that credits are awarded diminish the voluntary nature of the activity?

Volunteer administrators deal with these and other ethical questions and concerns on a daily basis within their organizations. The profession needs to address these issues on a global basis. The AVA has provided leadership in establishing performance standards for the profession that reflect ethical practice and provide a strong foundation for the future of volunteer administration.

Conclusion

The emergence of volunteer administration as a profession is marked by the leadership of the AVA, by the creation of standards of practice, and by the development of a strong literature base. The commitment of volunteer administrators to a high level of practice tends to be based on a sound personal philosophy of volunteerism. As in every profession, practitioners disagree about the nature and meaning of their practice, and these different conceptualizations suggest different visions of professionalism. Because volunteer administrators are challenged to make ethical judgments daily, they must rely on a consistent set of principles agreed on by the profession that aid them in responding to the moral dilemmas they confront in their practice.

Professional Ethics
in Volunteer Services
Administration

This code of Ethics and Standards, adopted at the Annual Meeting of the Association for Volunteer Administration in 1975, was copyrighted in 1978.

Declaration of Principles

Volunteer services administration exists to provide the leadership, structures and functions which facilitate the mobilization of human and other resources:

- to enable the meeting of human needs;
- to create a social climate which makes the meeting of human needs possible;
- to provide for the involvement of persons in the decision-making processes which affect them in social, economic, political, health and other realms;
- to contribute to creative and responsible social development and change;
- to enhance and extend the work of professional and other employed persons in certain service fields.

Principles

These principles have been adopted by the membership of the Association for Volunteer Administration to promote and maintain high standards of practice and ethical conduct among its members.

The Volunteer Services Administrator accepts the ethical responsibility to adhere to the following principles:

1. A Volunteer Services Administrator shall develop a personal coherent philosophy of volunteerism as a foundation for working with others in developing a volunteer program.
2. The Volunteer Services Administrator shall develop a volunteer program which will enhance the human dignity of all persons related to it.
3. The Volunteer Services Administrator shall promote the understanding and actualization of inherent mutual benefits for all parties involved in any act of volunteer service.
4. The Volunteer Services Administrator shall promote the involvement of persons in decision-making processes which affect them directly.
5. The Volunteer Services Administrator shall respect the privacy of individuals and safeguard information received as confidential.
6. The Volunteer Services Administrator shall develop a volunteer program which will enhance and extend the work of all professionals and other employed persons.
7. The Volunteer Services Administrator shall help create a social climate through which human needs can be met and human values enhanced.
8. The Volunteer Services Administrator shall contribute to the credibility of the profession in the eyes of those it serves.

AVA Certification Program in Volunteer Administration: Functional Areas and Competency Statements

Functional Areas and Competency Statements
Management I

I. Program Planning and Organization

This is the most basic task in volunteer administration. It involves the development of program goals consistent with the aims of the organization, the selection of objectives and alternative methods to reach those objectives. Effective planning and organization establishes the "map" that allows for the continuous operation of the program.

Program planning and organization requires that the volunteer administrator:

I.A.   Demonstrate knowledge of the agency/organization including its mission/purpose, its structure and the policies or regulations that affect its operation

Performance Criteria

I.A.1   describe to others the history and the mission of the agency/organization

I.A.2   develop and/or interpret to others a philosophy for the involvement of volunteers in the agency/

Note: The material in this resource is reprinted by permission of the Association for Volunteer Administration Board of Directors.

organization consistent with the aims of the organization

I.A.3   describe the actual operational structure of the agency/organization, including its:

3.a.   management structure

3.b.   relationship to its community, its client/consumer groups, other agencies, and its funding or regulating bodies

I.B.   Demonstrate the capability to engage in planning activities, armed with adequate information about the community and the agency/organization, which set the course of action for the volunteer program through goals, objectives and action plans

I.B.1   assess the community's potential volunteer resources (both human and material)

I.B.2   describe factors affecting the community resources in the geographic area served by the agency/organization (such as employment conditions, demographic patterns, socioeconomic patterns, and community concerns), and relate these factors to agency/organization planning for volunteers

I.B.3   describe broader trends which may affect agency planning for volunteers, such as: pending legislation; attitudes about volunteerism held by feminist groups, labor unions, and other professional groups; volunteer/career; and/or volunteer/academic credit concerns

I.B.4   identify needs and opportunities for volunteer services within the agency/organization and facilitate others (staff, volunteers and clients) in assisting with this process

I.B.5   write goal statements and objectives for the volunteer component of the agency/organization

I.B.6   manage the ordering of objectives, the setting of priorities and the concentration of resources to accomplish the selected objectives

I.B.7   assess resources necessary to accomplish objectives

I.B.8   present the rationale and justification of a budget in relationship to program needs and monetary request

I.B.9   work with the other groups (auxiliaries, foundations, and other community groups) to seek additional funding as necessary

I.B.10   monitor donated monies and materials to assure compliance with the donor's expectations (this may include individual gifts, as well as grants)

I.C.   Demonstrate the ability to make decisions

I.C.1   describe the nature of decisions and the range of possible actions which fall within the scope of the volunteer administrator's position

I.C.2   involve relevant persons (volunteers, clients, staff and/or outside consultants) in the diagnosis and management of decision making and problem solving situations

I.C.3   describe the agency/organization protocol in managing conflicts and making decisions

I.C.4   manage decision making situations

     4.a.   identify and clarify the nature of the problem and its causes

     4.b.   find alternative solutions

     4.c.   analyze/compare alternative solutions

     4.d.   select among alternatives and implement a course of action

     4.e.   monitor results of the selected course of action

I.D.   Establish structures and procedures to enable the smooth operation of the program

I.D.1   develop or implement systems for volunteer/staff/client communications to insure that:

     1.a.   client needs are solicited and reflected in services offered

        1.b.   staff needs are solicited and reflected in volunteer service opportunities

        1.c.   volunteers have channels to voice needs and interests

I.D.2   manage and develop systems to insure that:

        2.a.   records and reports are kept accurately and can be retrieved

        2.b.   volunteer job descriptions are written and opportunities are communicated

        2.c.   the entry and placement of volunteers is efficient and timely (includes volunteer applications, interviewing procedures, orientation and training program referral and placement systems)

        2.d.   volunteers, and staff who work with volunteers, receive recognition

I.E.   Assign the activities necessary to accomplish the goals and objectives of the program through delegation and coordination

I.E.1   clearly define tasks and responsibilities delegated to volunteers and staff carefully chosen for these responsibilities

I.E.2   provide support and supervision to volunteers

I.E.3   provide prompt, factual feedback to volunteers

I.E.4   establish channels for communication:

        4.a.   verbal communication channels, such as staff meetings, face-to-face contact, telephone calls

        4.b.   written communication channels, such as letters, reports, newsletters

I.F.   Demonstrate knowledge of the target population your agency/organization serves, including needs, strengths, limitations

I.F.1   display general knowledge of your target population, i.e., general characteristics

I.F.2   assess the specific needs of the target population

I.F.3   describe the strengths of this population

I.F.4   assess any specific limitations of the population, i.e., institutionalized or legally imposed restraints

I.F.5   involve the target population in determining their special needs, strengths and limitations, i.e., by advisory boards made up of representatives of target group, surveys, asking questions, etc.

Functional Areas and Competency Statements
Management II

II. Staffing and Directing

Selecting persons to do the jobs that need to be done *and* enabling their performance are staffing and directing responsibilities. This requires the design of job positions, the selection of personnel (both paid and volunteer), developing persons to do the jobs, guiding their performance and recognition for the services performed. "Planning and Organization" is the preparation of the program to meet its goals. "Staffing and Directing" is the actual implementation of the goals.

The staffing and directing function requires that the administrator:

II.A.   Demonstrate knowledge and expertise in planning and conducting successful recruitment campaigns

II.A.1   design a year-long recruitment campaign

II.A.2   develop and implement marketing techniques (such as exchanging value for value; identifying target populations and constituency groups) and apply them in a recruitment campaign

II.A.3   implement varied recruitment models (as appropriate to the target population and community situation), such as public speaking; media promotions; brochure development; and face-to-face contact

II.A.4   adapt recruitment strategies according to the trends affecting the community and influencing volunteer participation

II.A.5   involve staff, volunteers and other appropriate community people in implementing the recruitment campaign

II.A.6   articulate affirmative action requirements and implement recruitment plans to meet requirements

II.B.   Demonstrate knowledge and capability in selecting appropriate persons to fill positions

II.B.1   determine necessary criteria for various positions in advance of the interview

II.B.2   implement sound interviewing practices in the selection of volunteers

     2.a.   select an appropriate setting for the interview

     2.b.   use active listening to verbal and non-verbal messages

     2.c.   ask open ended questions

     2.d.   record pertinent information gained during the interview after the session

II.B.3   involve staff members and other volunteers in interviewing and selecting volunteers

II.B.4   design volunteer opportunities to meet the talents of volunteers if they are different from available openings (whenever possible)

II.B.5   interpret job descriptions and performance standards to volunteers prior to placement

II.B.6   describe the volunteer's rights and responsibilities

II.B.7   refer volunteers to other agencies if a position is not available for the particular individual

II.B.8   interpret the mission and purpose of the agency/organization and volunteer program to the candidate

II.B.9   match volunteers to positions based on the needs of the positions and the needs, motivations, and talents of the volunteers.

II.B.10   accumulate a successful history of matching volunteers to positions

II.B.11   interpret the needs and placement requirements of the various categories of volunteers involved in the program, such as the handicapped, older persons, minorities, youth, etc.

II.C.   Demonstrate knowledge of the growth and development needs of personnel and assure that these needs are addressed

II.C.1   identify and assure that volunteers are adequately prepared to fulfill their positions through:

    1.a.   orientation or preservice programs

    1.b.   in-service educational programs

    1.c.   ongoing supervision

II.C.2   involve volunteers, staff and educators in planning and implementing educational programs

II.C.3   maintain systems to identify and communicate information to volunteers and staff about educational programs external to the agency that might be beneficial to those persons

II.C.4   provide for orientation, training and/or consultation with staff in the utilization of volunteers

II.C.5   apply knowledge of the principles of career development to volunteer experiences

    5.a.   provide for the counsel/advisement of volunteers, assuring them of the program's concern for their ongoing personal development relative to their life, education and career within the aims of the program

    5.b.   assist volunteers in evaluating their volunteer experiences and personal growth, career exploration/development, and competencies acquired through volunteer experiences

    5.c.   identify community resources for assisting volunteers in exploring careers, identifying goals

II.C.6   assure that adequate records on volunteer experiences, training received at the agency, meaningful job records and data for references are kept

II.C.7   conduct performance appraisals with personnel on a regular basis

II.D.   Demonstrate the ability to motivate, communicate with, and lead volunteers and paid staff

II.D.1   interpret and apply motivational theories (such as need hierarchies, power, affiliation, achievement motivation) in work with volunteers through selecting appropriate:

1.a.   placements

1.b.   type of recognition accorded individual volunteers

1.c.   style of supervision

II.D.2   maintain ongoing channels of communication

II.D.3   insure longevity of volunteers in programs, or return of volunteers to program as in the case of students or persons performing special, time-limited projects

II.D.4   document the use of motivation and leadership skills in the accomplishment of program goals through volunteer personnel (if volunteers are well placed, motivated, supported and directed, they will be able to accomplish the tasks assigned to them)

II.E.   Recognize the accomplishment of personnel

II.E.1   conduct formal volunteer events well attended by invited volunteers and staff

II.E.2   develop articles, plaques, or other formal recognition featuring the involvement of volunteers, by name

II.E.3   write letters, notes, or other communications

which individually recognize the work of volunteers and/or staff who work with volunteers

II.E.4   promote volunteers to positions of greater responsibility or status

II.E.5   recognize staff relative to their effective utilization of and assistance to volunteers

II.F.   Facilitate the transition of volunteers to other life experiences

II.F.1   conduct exit interviews of volunteers choosing to terminate their involvement

II.F.2   create and/or maintain referral systems for volunteers to other agencies

II.F.3   establish and implement criteria for the termination of volunteers

Functional Areas and Competency Statements
Management III

III.   Controlling

This is the process of monitoring and evaluating the program to determine if events and activities have conformed to plans and produced the desired results. Documenting results and revising plans based on evaluation outcomes is part of the controlling process.

The controlling function requires that the volunteer administrator:

III.A.   Demonstrate the ability to monitor and evaluate total program results

III.A.1   develop and administer instruments designed to measure specific program results to program objectives

III.A.2   monitor volunteer attendance and/or attrition rates, and use this information in evaluating the effectiveness of placements and development programs

III.A.3   monitor the quantity and quality of volunteer use by various agency department areas and/or staff

III.A.4   conduct exit interviews with volunteers to determine reasons for leaving and to evaluate the volunteer's experience with the agency/organization

III.A.5   informally ask volunteers, staff, and clients about their experiences, concerns or problems as they relate to the volunteer program activities

III.A.6   monitor financial expenditures and make necessary adjustments to exercise fiscal control and responsibility

III.A.7   solicit and make ongoing constructive use of positive and negative feedback

III.B.   Demonstrate the ability to document program results and to apply this information in future planning

III.B.1   compile and interpret the results of measurement instruments and disseminate this information as appropriate

III.B.2   write reports describing volunteer program activities including appropriate figures on attendance and project outcomes

III.B.3   adjust program plans based on the results of formal and informal evaluation activities

III.B.4   document financial expenditures necessary to achieve program outcome

III.B.5   compile reports describing the degree to which the program meets standards, such as Hospital Accreditation or AVB accreditation standards for VAC's, when needed

III.B.6   maintain up-to-date personnel files on volunteers which include performance appraisals, training records and other appropriate information

Functional Areas and Competency Statements
Interpersonal Behavior IV

IV.   Individual, Group and Organizational Behavior
Volunteer programs exist within the larger context of the

agency/organization and the surrounding community. Maintaining working relationships in all of these areas is vital for successful program administration.

Individual, group and organizational behavior requires that the volunteer administrator:

IV.A   Demonstrate the ability to work effectively with many different segments of the population

IV.A.1   compile a demographic profile of volunteer and salaried work force (i.e., review of age, race, educational, etc., data) and analyze this information in relation to surrounding community

IV.A.2   maintain effective working relationships with volunteers, staff and community persons

Refer to the previous sections

IV.B.   Demonstrate a knowledge of group process and the ability to work with, and as a member of, groups

IV.B.1   serve productively on committees and/or boards

IV.B.2   form and/or convene committees, such as advisory committees, or boards of directors

IV.B.3   identify and interpret group goals and objectives

IV.B.4   create and follow agenda for committee meetings (as evidenced by committee minutes or reports)

IV.B.5   inform others of the progress or outcomes of committee meetings through written and/or verbal communications

IV.B.6   appoint appropriate persons to committees/ boards based on the desired goals and function of the group

IV.C.   Demonstrate knowledge of social organizations and dynamics of change

IV.C.1   describe other agencies and organizations within the community which interact with or affect your agency/organization and volunteer program, and explain the ways in which these agencies or groups affect your agency/organization and volunteer program

IV.C.2   describe the advocacy efforts of volunteers to your agency/organization and the broader community, particularly those advocacy efforts that affect your area of operation

IV.C.3   serve as a catalyst to help volunteers, clients, or community groups identify areas where change may be needed

IV.C.4   articulate factors creating blocks to change and suggest methods to facilitate change

Functional Areas and Competency Statements
Knowledge of the Profession V

V.   Grounding in the profession

A working knowledge of the field of volunteerism, its history, tradition, guiding philosophical background and current trends and issues separates the technician from the professional. A volunteer administrator who is grounded in the profession can:

V.A.   Demonstrate knowledge of external regulations affecting volunteerism

     V.A.1   describe tax deductions available to volunteers

     V.A.2   identify and interpret legislation, regulations and/or guidelines affecting your agency

     V.A.3   identify sources for procuring pertinent governmental information

     V.A.4   identify and interpret legislation, regulations and/or guidelines affecting voluntary action in general

     V.A.5   interpret the regulations governing lobbying done by voluntary organizations

V.B.   Demonstrate knowledge of the history and philosophy of voluntary action and trends affecting volunteerism

     V.B.1   articulate and interpret to others a philosophy

of voluntary action and its relationship to a democratic society and to service institutions

V.B.2 describe the history and scope of volunteer involvement in one's agency/organization

V.B.3 interpret the AVA "Professional Ethics in Volunteer Services Administration" and demonstrate its relationship to one's program in at least two ways

V.B.4 articulate a personal philosophy* on issues in contemporary volunteer services administration such as stipends for service; academic or employment credit for volunteer work; feminist movement and its effect on volunteerism; and corporation and labor views on volunteerism

V.C. Demonstrate knowledge of the profession of volunteer administration

V.C.1 identify the professional groups for volunteer administrators in one's local geographic region and at the national level

V.C.2 document participation in a professional group or association

V.C.3 identify periodicals in volunteer administration

V.C.4 identify and describe trends in educational programs for volunteer administration

V.C.5 attend workshops and conferences on volunteerism

V.C.6 read professional materials related to volunteer program management

---

*This philosophy should demonstrate an awareness of both sides of the issues and one's personal position on the issue.

References

Aaker, D. A., and Day, G. S. *Marketing Research.* New York: Wiley, 1983.

Allen, N. "The Role of Social and Organizational Factors in the Evaluation of Volunteer Programs." *Evaluation and Program Planning,* 1987, *10*(3), 257-263.

American Field Service Center for the Study of Intercultural Learning. *Assessing the Candidate.* Theory into Practice Series, No. 1. New York: AFS Intercultural Programs, 1984.

Arthur, D. *Recruiting, Interviewing, Selecting and Orienting New Employees.* New York: American Management Association, 1986.

Baker, B. J., and Murawski, K. "A Method for Measuring Paid Staff Support for Volunteer Involvement." *Journal of Voluntary Action Research,* 1986, *15*(3), 60-64.

Bennis, W. "The 4 Competencies of Leadership." *Training and Development Journal,* Aug. 1984, *38*(8), 14-19.

Bennis, W. "Learning Some Basic Truisms About Leadership." *National Forum,* Winter 1991, *71*(1), 12-15.

Birnbaum, R. "Why It's Difficult to Increase Productivity." *AGB Reports,* 1991, *33*(2), 6-11.

Bramhall, M. "How to Prevent Volunteer Burnout." *Voluntary Action Leadership,* Winter 1985, pp. 20-23.

Brown, E. P., and Zahrly, J. "Nonmonetary Rewards for Skilled Volunteer Labor: A Look at Crisis Intervention Volunteers."

Nonprofit and Voluntary Sector Quarterly, Summer 1989, *18*(2), 167–176.

Brudney, J. C. *Fostering Volunteer Programs in the Public Sector.* San Francisco: Jossey-Bass, 1990.

Burke, R. J., and Lindsay, L. "Motivation and Goal Setting." In L. F. Moore (ed.), *Motivating Volunteers.* Vancouver, B.C.: Vancouver Volunteer Centre, 1985.

Caraway, J., and Van Gilder, J. "The Role of Lay Volunteers in a Community Hypertension Control Program." *Journal of Voluntary Action Research,* Apr.-Sept. 1985, *14*(2–3), 134–141.

Chambre, I. M. "Recruiting Black and Hispanic Volunteers: A Qualitative Study of Organizations' Experience." *Journal of Volunteer Administration,* Fall 1982, *1*(1), 3–10.

Colomy, P., Chen, H., and Andrews, G. L. "Situational Facilities and Volunteer Work." *Journal of Volunteer Administration,* Winter 1987, *6*(2), 20–25.

Cronk, V. M. "If It Acts Like a Manager, It Must Be a Manager." *Journal of Volunteer Administration,* Fall 1982, *6*(2), 11–17.

Curtis, K. M. "Philosophy of Volunteerism." *Journal of Volunteer Administration,* Winter 1986, *5*(2), 23.

Curtis, K. M., and Fisher, J. C. "Valuing Volunteers: A Naturalistic Approach." *Journal of Volunteer Administration,* Fall 1989, *8*(1), 11–20.

Dailey, R. C. "Understanding Organizational Commitment for Volunteers: Empirical and Managerial Implications." *Journal of Voluntary Action Research,* Jan.-Mar. 1986, *15*(1), 19–31.

Deal, T. E., and Kennedy, A. A. *Corporate Cultures: The Rites and Rituals of Corporate Life.* Reading, Mass.: Addison-Wesley, 1982.

Deci, E. L., Connell, J. P., and Ryan, R. M. "Self-Determinism in a Work Organization." *Journal of Applied Psychology,* 1981, *74*(4), 580–590.

DeNisi, A. S., Robbins, T., and Cafferty, T. P. "Organization of Information for Performance Appraisals: Role of Diary-Keeping." *Journal of Applied Psychology,* 1989, *74*(1), 124–129.

Drucker, P. F. *Management. Tasks. Responsibilities. Practices.* New York: HarperCollins, 1974.

Drucker, P. F. "What Business Can Learn from Nonprofits." *Harvard Business Review,* July-Aug. 1989, *67*(4), 88-93.

Dugan, K. W. "Ability and Effort Attributions: How Much Do They Affect How Managers Communicate Performance Feedback Information?" *Academy of Management Journal,* 1989, *32*(1), 87-114.

Eckles, R. W., Carmichael, R. L., and Sarchet, B. R. *Supervisory Management.* New York: Wiley, 1983.

Elkins, R. L., and Cohen, C. R. "A Comparison of the Effects of Prejob Training and Job Experience on Nonprofessional Telephone Crisis Counselors." *Suicide and Life-Threatening Behavior,* Summer 1982, *12*(2), 84-89.

Ellis, S. J. *From the Top Down.* Philadelphia: Energize Associates, 1986.

Ellis, S. J. "On Volunteers." *Nonprofit Times,* May 26, 1991, p.26.

Ellis, S. J., and Noyes, K. H. *By the People: A History of Americans as Volunteers.* (Rev. ed.) San Francisco: Jossey-Bass, 1990.

English, G. "Tuning Up for Performance Management." *Training and Development Journal,* April 1991, *45*(4), 56-60.

Ensman, R. "Recruiting Volunteers Through an Annual Campaign." *Voluntary Action Leadership,* Winter 1984, pp. 28-31.

Filinson, R. "A Model for Church-Based Services for Frail Elderly Persons and Their Families." *Gerontologist,* Aug. 1988, *28*(4), 483-485.

Fiset, J. C., Freeman, D. J., Ilsley, P. J., and Snow, B. R. "Adult Learning in Volunteer Settings: A Neglected Connection." *Proceedings of the Twenty-Eighth Annual Adult Education Research Conference.* Laramie: University of Wyoming, 1987.

Francies, G. R. "The Volunteer Needs Profile: A Tool for Reducing Turnover." *Journal of Volunteer Administration,* Summer 1983, *1*(4), 17-33.

Fulmer, R. M., and Franklin, S. G. *Supervision.* New York: Macmillan, 1982.

Gamm, L., and Kassab, C. "Productivity Assessment of Volunteer Programs in Not-for-Profit Human Services Organizations." *Journal of Voluntary Action Research,* 1983, *12*(3), 23-38.

Gardner, J. E. *Training the New Supervisor.* New York: American Management Association, 1980.

Gaston, N. "Easy Does It: Initiating a Performance Evaluation Process in an Existing Volunteer Program." *Journal of Volunteer Administration,* Fall 1989, *8*(1), 27–30.

Geber, B. "Managing Volunteers." *Training,* June 1991, *28*(6), 21–26.

George, C. *Supervision in Action: The Art of Managing Others.* Reston, Va.: Reston, 1982.

Gidron, B. "Sources of Job Satisfaction Among Service Volunteers." *Journal of Voluntary Action Research,* Jan.-Mar. 1983, *12*(1), 20–35.

Giles, W. F., and Mossholder, K. W. "Employee Reactions to Contextual and Session Components of Performance Appraisal." *Journal of Applied Psychology,* 1990, *75*(4), 371–377.

Hayslip, B., and Walling, M. L. "Impact of Hospice Volunteer Training on Death Anxiety and Locus of Control." *Omega,* 1985–1986, *16*(3), 243–245.

Heidrich, K. W. "Volunteers' Life Styles: Market Segmentation Based on Volunteer's Role Choice." *Voluntary Sector Quarterly,* Spring 1990, *19*(1).

Henderson, K. A. "The Motivation of Men and Women in Volunteering." *Journal of Volunteer Administration,* Spring 1983, *1*(3), 20–24.

Hersey, P., and Blanchard, K. H. *Management of Organizational Behavior.* Englewood Cliffs, N.J.: Prentice-Hall, 1982.

Herzberg, F. *Work and the Nature of Man.* New York: World, 1966.

Herzberg, F., Mausner, B., and Synderman, B. *The Motivation to Work.* New York: Wiley, 1959.

Hodgkinson, V. A., and Weitzman, M. S. *Dimensions of the Independent Sector: A Statistical Profile.* (3rd ed.) Washington, D.C.: Independent Sector, 1989.

Houle, C. O. *Continuing Learning in the Professions.* San Francisco: Jossey-Bass, 1980.

Hoy, W. K., and Miskel, C. G. *Educational Administration.* (2nd ed.) New York: Random House, 1982.

Ilsley, P. J. "The Voluntary Sector and Adult Education." In S. B. Merriam and P. M. Cunningham (eds.), *Handbook of Adult and Continuing Education.* San Francisco: Jossey-Bass, 1989.

Ilsley, P. J. *Enhancing the Volunteer Experience.* San Francisco: Jossey-Bass, 1990.

Independent Sector. "Gallup Survey Reveals Sharp Rises in Giving and Volunteering." *Voluntary Action Leadership,* Fall 1990, pp. 13-15.

Institute for Financial Education. "Building Work Relationships." In Institute for Financial Education, *Supervisory Personnel Management.* Chicago: Institute for Financial Education, 1988.

Kane-Williams, E., Salisbury, Z. T., and Benson, L. "Training of Persons for the Delivery of the Staying Healthy After Fifty Program." *Health Education Quarterly,* Winter 1989, *16*(4), 473-483.

Karn, G. N. "Money Talks: A Guide to Establishing the True Dollar Value of Volunteer Time, Part I." *Journal of Volunteer Administration,* Winter 1982-1983, *1*(2), 1-17.

Kotter, J. P. *A Force for Change. How Leadership Differs from Management.* New York: Free Press, 1990.

Langer, G. M. "Future Perfect." *Currents,* Apr. 1987, *13*(4), 18-22.

Lawson, S. "Philosophy of Volunteerism." *Journal of Volunteer Administration,* Winter 1986, *5*(2), 19.

Likert, R. *New Patterns of Management.* New York: McGraw-Hill, 1961.

Lynch, R. "Designing Volunteer Jobs for Results." *Voluntary Action Leadership,* Summer 1983, pp. 20-23.

Lynch, R. "Targeted Volunteer Recruiting." *Voluntary Action Leadership,* Fall, 1990, pp. 24-33.

McClelland, D.C. *Human Motivation.* Glenview, Ill.: Scott, Foresman, 1985.

McCurley, S., and Lynch, R. *Essential Volunteer Management.* Downers Grove, Ill.: VM Systems and Heritage Arts, 1989.

Macduff, N. *Volunteer Recruiting and Retention.* Walla Walla, Wash.: Macduff/Bunt Associates, 1985.

Macduff, N. "Assessing Your Supervisory Skills." *Voluntary Action Leadership,* Fall 1986, pp. 18-20.

Macduff, N. "Three Steps to Successful Screening of Volunteers." *Voluntary Action Leadership,* Fall-Winter 1987, pp. 26-27.

Macduff, N. "Episodic Volunteers: Reality for the Future." *Voluntary Action Leadership,* Spring 1990, pp. 15-17.

Macduff, N. "Sustenance: Providing Support for the Short-Term

Volunteer." *Voluntary Action Leadership*, Winter 1991, pp. 22-24.

McGregor, D. "The Human Side of Enterprise." In D. McGregor, *Leadership and Motivation*. Cambridge, Mass.: MIT Press, 1966.

Marsick, V. J. "A New Era in Staff Development." In V. J. Marsick (ed.), *Enhancing Staff Development in Diverse Settings*, New Directions for Continuing Education Series, no. 38. San Francisco: Jossey-Bass, 1988.

Marx, M. "Role Review." *Voluntary Action Leadership*, Fall 1981, pp. 22-26.

Maslow, A. H. *Motivation and Personality*. (2nd ed.) New York: HarperCollins, 1970.

Mason, J. "Philosophy of Volunteerism." *Journal of Volunteer Administration*, Winter 1986, 5(2), 25.

Miller, R. W. "Extending University Resources in Support of Volunteer Development: Evaluation of a Pilot Effort." *Journal of Voluntary Action Research*, July-Mar. 1986, 15(1), 100-115.

Miller, R. W. "Using Evaluation to Support the Program Advisory Function: A Case Study of Evaluator–Program Advisory Committee Collaboration." *Evaluation and Program Planning*, 1987, 10(3), 281-288.

Nehnevajsa, J., and Kareletz, A. P. *Perspectives on Motivation of Volunteers: Pittsburgh SMSA*. Pittsburgh: Center for Urban Research, University of Pittsburgh, 1976.

Nestor, L. G. "Hispanic Americans: Tapping a New Volunteer Market." *Voluntary Action Leadership*, Fall 1984, pp. 19-25.

Nestor, L. G. "Managing Cultural Diversity in Volunteer Organizations." *Voluntary Action Leadership*, Winter 1991, pp. 18-19.

Nestor, L. G., and Fillichio, C. "Valuing Diversity." *Voluntary Action Leadership*, Winter 1991, pp. 20-21.

Newmann, M., and Montgomery, B. "Screening Volunteers with Vulnerable Persons." *Volunteers Move Minnesota*, 1989, 14(1), 5-6.

O'Connell, B. "America's Voluntary Spirit." *Journal of Volunteer Administration*, Spring 1986, 4(3), 16-20.

Parkum, K. H. "Instrumental and Expressive Dimensions of the Impact of Volunteers on Hospital Patients." *Journal of Voluntary Action Research*, Apr.-Sept. 1985, 14(2-3), 123-132.

Patton, M. Q. *Utilization-Focused Evaluation.* (2nd ed.) Newbury Park, Calif.: Sage, 1986.

Patton, M. Q. "Beyond Evaluation Myths." *Adult Learning,* Oct. 1991, *3*(2), 9-10, 28.

Pearce, J. L. "Leading and Following Volunteers: Implications for a Changing Society." *Journal of Applied Behavioral Science,* 1982, *18*(3), 385-394.

Pearce, J. L. "Participation in Voluntary Associations: How Membership in a Formal Organization Changes the Rewards of Participation." In D. H. Smith and J. Van Til (eds.), *International Perspectives on Voluntary Action Research.* Washington, D.C.: University Press of America, 1983.

Pelligrino, E. D., Veatch, R. M., and Langan, J. P. *Ethics, Trust, and the Professions.* Washington, D.C.: Georgetown University Press, 1991.

Peterson, R. D. "The Anatomy of Cost-Effectiveness Analysis." *Evaluation Review,* 1986, *10*(1), 29-44.

Phillips, M. "Motivation and Expectation in Successful Volunteerism." *Journal of Voluntary Action Research,* Apr.-Sept. 1982, *11*(2), 118-125.

Posavac, E. J., and Carey, R. G. *Program Evaluation, Methods and Case Studies.* (3rd ed.) Englewood Cliffs, N.J.: Prentice-Hall, 1989.

Prien, E. P., and Schippman, J. S. "Screening and Selecting Staff for the Nonprofit Organization." In E. W. Anthes and J. Cronin (eds.), *Personnel Matters in the Nonprofit Organization.* West Memphis and Hampton, Ark.: Independent Community Consultants, 1987.

Rehnborg, S. J. "Performance-Based Assessment Program for the Certification of Volunteer Administrators." Paper sponsored by the Association for Volunteer Administration, Boulder, Colo., Jan. 1982.

Reilly, A. J., and Jones, J. E. "Team Building." *1974 Annual Handbook for Group Facilitators.* La Jolla, Calif.: University Associates, 1974.

Robinson, R. D. *An Introduction to Helping Adults Learn and Change.* Milwaukee: Omnibook, 1983.

Saxon, J. P., and Sawyer, H. W. "A Systematic Approach for Volunteer Assignment and Retention." *Journal of Volunteer Administration,* Summer 1984, *2*(4), 39–45.

Scheier, I. H. *Exploring Volunteer Space: The Recruiting of a Nation.* Boulder, Colo.: VOLUNTEER: The National Center for Citizen Involvement, 1980a.

Scheier, I. H. "The Task Enrichment System: A First Outline." *Volunteer Administration,* 1980b, *13*(3), 15–26.

Schindler-Rainman, E. "Looking Ahead: Mobilizing Sources and Resources for the Future." *Voluntary Action Leadership,* Summer 1986, pp. 28–32.

Schindler-Rainman, E. "Administration of Volunteer Programs." In T. D. Connor (ed.), *The Nonprofit Organization Handbook.* New York: McGraw-Hill, 1988.

Sherrott, R. "Fifty Volunteers." In S. Hatch (ed.), *Volunteers: Patterns, Meanings and Motives.* Berkhamsted, Herts, England: Volunteer Centre, 1983.

Sills, D. *The Volunteer.* New York: Free Press, 1957.

Skillingstad, C. "Philosophy of Volunteerism." *Journal of Volunteer Administration,* Winter 1986, *5*(2), 21.

Smith, M. P. "Taking Volunteerism into the 21st Century: Some Conclusions from the American Red Cross VOLUNTEER 2000 Study." *Journal of Volunteer Administration,* Fall 1989, *8*(1), 3–10.

Stone, J. R., and Hansen-Stone, J. "Marketing Volunteerism: A Program Development Perspective." *Journal of Volunteer Administration,* Fall 1987, *6*(1), 14–24.

Stubblefield, H. W., and Miles, L. "Administration of Volunteer Programs as a Career: What Role for Higher Education?" *Journal of Voluntary Action Research,* 1986, *15*, 4–12.

Sues, A. M., and Wilson, P. A. "Developing a Hospital's Volunteer Program." *Health and Social Work,* Winter 1987, *12*(1), 13–20.

Tremper, C. R. *Reconsidering Legal Liability and Insurance for Nonprofit Organizations.* Lincoln, Nebr.: Law Education Services, 1989.

Utterback, J., and Heyman, S. R. "An Examination of Methods in the Evaluation of Volunteer Programs." *Evaluation and Program Planning,* 1984, *7*(3), 229–235.

Vineyard, S. "Recruiting and Retaining Volunteers." *Journal of Volunteer Administration,* Spring 1984, *2*(3), 23–28.

Vroom, V. H. *Work and Motivation.* New York: Wiley, 1964.

Waldner, M. "Philosophy of Volunteerism." *Journal of Volunteer Administration,* Winter 1986, *5*(2), 29.

Watts, A. D., and Edwards, P. K. "Recruiting and Retaining Human Service Volunteers: An Empirical Analysis." *Journal of Voluntary Action Research,* July-Sept. 1983, *12*(3), 9–22.

Weinstein, A. *Market Segmentation.* Chicago: Probus, 1987.

Wilensky, H. L. "The Professionalization of Everyone?" *American Journal of Sociology,* 1964, *70,* 137–158.

Wilkinson, H. J., and Wilkinson, J. W. "Evaluation of a Hospice Volunteer Training Program." *Omega,* 1986-1987, *17*(3), 263–275.

Wilson, M. *The Effective Management of Volunteer Programs.* Boulder, Colo.: Volunteer Management Association, 1976.

Wilson, M. "Reversing the Resistance of Staff to Volunteers." *Voluntary Action Leadership,* Spring 1981, p. 21.

Wilson, M. "The New Frontier: Volunteer Management Training." *Training and Development Journal,* July 1984, *38*(7), 50–52.

Index

203